What Readers Are Saying About Dr. Robert Lesslie's Books...

Angels in the ER

"This is a heartwarming book that I c ___ ___ put down. Makes one really think what it means to take care of those in need with compassion and patience—and adds a bit of humor to help you through the day."

"These marvelous medical stories with a Christian message touched my heart deeply. The book's ending could not have been more perfect."

"Simply amazing—a definite read for this tired ER nurse who sometimes loses sight of why we do this job!"

Angels on Call

"Love this series of books! Great action from the first lines. Especially good for anyone involved in (or wishing to be involved in) any type of emergency response or medical field."

"These stories are believable, heartwarming, and sometimes tragic at the same time. They give a true perspective of what it is like to deal with people at their most vulnerable time."

Angels and Heroes

"These true-life accounts remind us how special paramedics, doctors, firemen, and policemen are as many of them put their lives on the line for each of us every day and do everything possible to save lives. They truly are angels and heroes."

"I chose this book because I'm a firefighter, and it's one of the best I've ever read. I would recommend this to anyone looking for awesome stories of what first responders deal with every day."

Angels on the Night Shift

"I have read every collection of stories Dr. Lesslie has published. They are spiritual and uplifting but not sappy or preachy. I recommend this to the Christian, the ER buff, and the emergency services guru."

"A look at the real heart of an ER doc, the staff, and the interesting cases they confront. I want to read all of Dr. Lesslie's books!"

Miracles in the ER

"I love this author. Some of his stories are humorous, and some will make you cry. I love the short stories for when I only have time for a quick read."

"Very well-written book—entertaining and filled with examples of the effect of prayer and the hand of God in the ER. It will leave you with many points to meditate on."

Notes from a Doctor's Pocket

"Dr. Lesslie's short stories of ER patients sometimes end positively and sometimes not, but there is always a feeling that God is there in the ER with the patients and staff. If you like medical stories with God in attendance, you will enjoy this book and all of Dr. Lesslie's books."

ANGELS
to the
RESCUE

Robert Lesslie, MD

HARVEST HOUSE PUBLISHERS
EUGENE, OREGON

Cover design by Left Coast Design

Cover Image © blurAZ / Shutterstock

Interior design by Chad Dougherty

ANGELS TO THE RESCUE
Copyright © 2017 Robert D. Lesslie, MD
Published by Harvest House Publishers
Eugene, Oregon 97402
www.harvesthousepublishers.com

ISBN 978-0-7369-6695-5 (pbk.)
ISBN 978-0-7369-6696-2 (eBook)

Library of Congress Cataloging-in-Publication Data
Names: Lesslie, Robert D., 1951- author.
Title: Angels to the rescue / Robert D. Lesslie.
Description: Eugene, Oregon : Harvest House Publishers, [2017]
Identifiers: LCCN 2017001906 (print) | LCCN 2017009718 (ebook) | ISBN 9780736966955 (paperback) | ISBN 9780736966962 (ebook)
Subjects: LCSH: Hospitals—Emergency services—Popular works. | Emergency medical personnel—Popular works. | BISAC: RELIGION / Christian Life / General.
Classification: LCC RA975.5.E5 L479 2017 (print) | LCC RA975.5.E5 (ebook) | DDC 362.18—dc23
LC record available at https://lccn.loc.gov/2017001906

Printed in the United States of America

17 18 19 20 21 22 23 24 25 / BP-CD / 10 9 8 7 6 5 4 3

Dedicated to the men and women
who work "in the trenches."
Police officers, firefighters, paramedics, nurses,
and the many others who,
with no regard for their own safety,
come to our rescue.
Thank you.

The Emergency Room

Contents

1: 180 11

2: The Ghost 23

3: The Widow-Maker 33

4: In the Nick of Time 45

5: Maybelle Jenkins 55

6: A Seed Planted 63

7: A Charmed Life 73

8: Another Look 87

9: Pull Over! 97

10: Big Stan 109

11: It's Not Always Black-and-White 121

12: Into the Storm 133

13: Amber Alert 147

14: The Deep, Dark Woods 157

15: "911—What's Your Emergency?" 169

16: Three…Four…Five 183

17: Let Me Take a Listen 193

18: Getting It Right 201

19: What's in the Well Comes Up in the Bucket 211

20: Cynthia 221

21: The Choice 229

22: The Ascent 241

"Papa…are there really such things as angels? And what do they do?"

I tucked the blanket under my seven-year-old grandson's chin and stroked his silky blond hair. It was his bedtime, but he was wide awake. That was a good thing, since this was going to take a while. Many faces of men and women I had known and worked with flashed through my mind. Telling their stories wasn't always easy and shouldn't be hurried.

"Yes, Christian, there *are* angels. And I've known a few."

> *Since it is so likely that they will meet cruel enemies,*
> *let them at least have heard of brave knights*
> *and heroic courage.*
>
> C.S. Lewis

1

180

Everybody has a story. Give them a chance, and they'll tell you.

W e're going to need something to sedate the guy back in Minor Trauma A." Lori dropped the man's chart to the countertop and walked behind the nurses' station to wash her hands. "Something strong."

"Willie Childers?" Amy asked. "The twenty-year-old Officer Jones just brought in?"

"Yes." Lori shook her head and dried her hands. "He was completely calm when we took him to the back. I was wondering why Elton kept the man's cuffs on and why the other highway patrolman kept a hand on his shoulder. I'm glad they were there though, 'cause when I asked him to get up on the stretcher, he exploded. Started kicking and screaming. It was all we could do to get him on the stretcher and on his back. If he does that again, he's going to hurt himself or someone else."

"So that's the ruckus we heard down the hallway," I observed. "Thought it was a party or something going on."

"It was a party, all right." Lori straightened her shirt and walked around the counter. "A PCP party, by the looks of it. Elton and his partner responded to a car in a ditch out on the interstate and found this guy sitting on the bank, staring at the moon. He had a couple of outbursts with them, but they managed to get him cuffed and into the patrol car. Now he's our problem—until we can get him medically cleared."

"Well, let's go see if we can do that."

I grabbed the clipboard of Minor Trauma A and headed down the hallway.

Elton Jones and his partner flanked the stretcher in the left-rear corner of the room. A young man was lying there shirtless with his eyes closed.

"What you got here, Elton?" I asked quietly, not wanting to startle the moon-staring young man.

I stood beside the highway patrolman, and my eyes were drawn to his always impeccable and neatly pressed uniform. The top two buttons of his long-sleeved shirt were gone, and his right shirtsleeve was ripped to the elbow, its tattered edges dangling from his forearm.

He looked at me and then at his torn sleeve. He shifted his body and moved his arm out of my view, but I had seen them—the burn scars that began at his wrist, encircled his forearm, and disappeared above his elbow.

Lori had been right. PCP was indeed the culprit in Minor Trauma and the cause of the young man's bizarre behavior. Actually the culprit was his bad decision making. The PCP was just an instrument.

"Think we'll be able to take him to the jail this evening?"

Elton stood beside me at the nurses' station, making some notes on his report ledger.

"We're waiting on a couple of things to come back from the lab," I told him. "But he's calming down and should be stable enough. What kind of charges do you have on him?"

"Well, for one thing, he was driving under the influence. I'm just glad he didn't run into someone, because for the second thing, he was driving south on I-77 in the northbound lane."

"What?" My head spun around and I stared at the patrolman. "He was driving on the wrong side of the interstate?"

Elton nodded his head and sighed. "Not the first time that's happened."

He glanced down at his right forearm and looked at the burn scar. "It's happened before."

"This is 911 Dispatch. We have reports of a vehicle speeding on I-77." Elton Jones cocked his head and listened. He was on Highway 21, not far from the interstate. But this sounded like a routine call, something the local police or county sheriff's deputies could handle.

"And the vehicle is heading south in a northbound lane."

Elton glanced in his rearview mirror, slammed on his breaks, and executed a quick and smooth U-turn. This was something different. A disaster waiting to happen.

He flipped on his lights and siren and headed toward the interstate.

"You sure you don't want me to drive?"

Gracie Lyon was in the front passenger seat, trying to stay awake. It was midnight, and she and her friend had been on the road for three hours, headed home to Michigan from a week at Myrtle Beach.

"You're kidding, right?" Heather Anderson glanced at her friend and smiled. "You can barely keep your eyes open. Go back to sleep."

"No, really." Gracie's persistence was halfhearted. "I can drive if you want." She yawned again and closed her eyes.

The two were roommates at Michigan State—friends since grade school. Carefree and sunburned, they planned to stop for the night on the other side of Charlotte, about 45 minutes away.

Heather shifted in her seat, adjusted the rearview mirror, and watched mile marker 65 speed by.

Elton was on the radio, asking if there were any other patrol cars in the area. There was a bad wreck on Highway 5—the other side of the county—and most of the sheriff's deputies were already on the scene or on the way.

Nobody answered his request for help.

How do I stop this guy before he kills someone?

Elton was almost on the interstate. Depending on the speed of the vehicle, the driver could be anywhere between three and ten miles up the road—headed his way. Or maybe he had figured out he was in the wrong lane and turned around. Not likely. It was after midnight, and the chances of alcohol or another intoxicant being involved were pretty high.

He took the exit onto I-77 and was immediately thankful. Scant traffic, with only a few moving lights visible in both directions.

Think, man. How am I going to do this?

With help from other police and highway patrolmen, a plan could quickly be put together blocking traffic heading north and isolating the wayward driver. But could Elton find the help?

He passed a pickup truck, its driver nodding and waving as the officer sped by.

Elton slowed and motioned for the driver to pull over.

Every minute mattered, and Elton didn't get out of the patrol car but pulled alongside the stopped truck.

"You're fine," he told the confused driver. "We've got a problem up ahead, and I need you to pull over and stay here until I come back. Got it?"

The man nodded and pulled onto the shoulder.

Elton sped off, searching the road ahead for other taillights. Clear.

"Elton, what's going on?"

The voice on the radio was faint and scratchy, but still recognizable as Chad Stevens, another patrolman on duty in the county.

"Where are you, Chad?"

"Highway 9, between Chester and the interstate. You need some help?"

Elton told him what was happening, and they put together a hasty plan.

Chad was to drive north on the interstate, pick a spot beyond one of the big interchanges, and stop traffic at that point. He had some flares and reflective cones, but it would still be risky. Elton would keep heading north, locate the driver, and get him or her to pull off the road—he hoped.

"This is 911 Dispatch. We just had another report of the same vehicle still heading south in a northbound lane. Weaving in the road and nearly running a trucker off the highway."

"We need to hurry," Chad said. In the radio's background, Elton heard the first wail of the patrolman's siren. "Good luck."

Good luck? I'll need more than that.

So much for the driver realizing his error and turning around.

A couple of mile markers passed by in a blur, yet Elton could see no other taillights on the road. And no headlights coming his way. Not yet. He tried to remember his training but couldn't come up with a plan that had even a small chance of stopping this guy. There aren't many options when it comes to a one-on-one challenge like this. He had to get the guy off the road, but how? Once he saw the car, he could turn around, catch up with him, and force him off the road. Risky, especially if there were other cars coming. Chad could block the interstate but not the entrances. And all it would take would be one vehicle getting through to create a potential disaster.

More taillights up ahead. Elton knew he didn't have time to pull this car over, as he had done with the truck. Too little highway between him and the oncoming car.

He sped by the Toyota Camry, its driver twisting her head in his direction, wide-eyed.

"Elton, this is Chad. I'm at marker 74 and have got things stopped. Should be okay here, but the on-ramps are still open."

"Good work, Chad. I'm—"

Headlights, bearing down on him.

Elton dropped the radio and white-knuckled the steering wheel. The thought of playing chicken—forcing the driver off the road—flitted through his brain and was gone. That wasn't going to work.

The headlights straddled the middle of the road but then suddenly swerved to one side. Elton jerked the wheel, narrowly missing the late-model Ford Explorer that roared past him. He slammed on his brakes, reversed direction, and began chasing the Explorer.

He picked up the radio and pressed the speaker button.

"Chad, I'm right behind the guy. Ford Explorer, doing at least 90."

"Don't do anything crazy, Elton."

What could be crazier than this?

The driver of the Toyota he had just passed was paying attention, saw the two sets of headlights, and drove off the road and up a grassy bank. Elton roared past, thankful that one collision had been avoided. Now how would he stop the Explorer?

Heather Anderson was on a long, straight stretch of highway. A burst of light flashed in her rearview mirror, and she looked up at it. Then another—flames of some sort, a mile or so behind her.

"Gracie, did you…" Her friend was leaning against the passenger door, fast asleep.

Heather chuckled and looked again in the mirror. Darkness.

Chad's flares were doing their work, obscured now behind a rise in the highway.

Elton was right behind the Explorer. He blew his horn and flashed his lights. No response. This guy wasn't going to stop. He thought about ramming him from the back. That might cause the driver to lose control, spin out, and crash. Not the best outcome, but Elton was running out of time—out of seconds.

The Explorer accelerated, creating space between the two vehicles. Elton made up his mind. He steered left, leaving plenty of room between him and the Explorer. Then he floored the patrol car, easily passing the Ford. As he sailed past, Elton glanced at the driver. Young guy, mid to late twenties, with a scruffy beard. As Elton passed, the driver rolled his head in the officer's direction, smiled, and gave a slow wave of his hand. This guy wasn't going to stop. Not on his own.

Elton whipped his car in front of the Explorer and kept his eyes glued on the rearview mirror. He thought about gradually slowing down but thought better of it. The guy would only ram him and probably send the patrol car off the road. But how long could this go on? Chad Stevens was up ahead with his roadblock, but if the Explorer got through, how many unsuspecting drivers were beyond him? No, something had to happen, and soon.

As if reading Elton's mind, the driver of the Explorer feigned to veer to the left, causing Elton to adjust his position. When he did, the Explorer swerved to the right and was past him—barreling down the interstate.

"Son of a gun!" Elton yanked his steering wheel and accelerated.

Up ahead lay a long stretch of highway, dark and disappearing over a distant hill. But then...headlights.

Elton's body stiffened and his hands clenched the steering wheel. *Where did they come from? How did they get past Chad's roadblock?*

It didn't matter. Elton had to get this guy off the highway. He pulled even with the Explorer and motioned for the driver to pull over. This time he didn't even look in Elton's direction.

A quick glance up the road...the headlights were closing in on them.

Elton pulled just ahead of the Explorer and made his move. In the split second he had to make up his mind, he knew what had to happen. It might mean his own death, but he had to hit the front end of the Explorer and guide it off the road. At 90 miles an hour, he knew anything could happen.

The oncoming headlights were only seconds away and headed straight for them. Elton pulled hard on the steering wheel and braced himself.

So this is it. This is what it feels like, knowing that you are about to die and can't do anything about it.
He took a deep breath, waited for the impact and...nothing. The road beside him was empty, and he jerked the patrol car back into the highway.

The driver of the Explorer had slammed on his brakes, veered to the left, and was aiming at the approaching headlights.

In the vehicle just up ahead, Heather couldn't believe what she was seeing.

"Gracie! Wake up!"

Elton was back on the highway, heading straight for the Explorer. There would be no second chance.

It all happened so fast—a sort of bizarre dance, played out in the middle of a dark and deserted stretch of interstate. Elton rammed his patrol car into the side of the Explorer, causing the Ford's right-front and rear wheels to rise in the air. The Explorer and patrol car clutched each other, spun a full 360 degrees, and then separated and rolled away in different directions. A grotesque and deadly dance.

Through his shattered driver's window, Elton saw the other vehicle—a dark SUV—somehow escape unstruck. Suddenly it spun out of control, off the highway, and into a steep bank. It strained to climb the grassy hill, came to a slow stall, then began its descent, rolling over three times before coming to rest on the paved shoulder.

Elton scrambled out of his patrol car and ran toward the SUV. Fifty yards up the road, illuminated by Elton's high beams, the Explorer had come to a twisted and contorted stop. It was upside down, its wheels still spinning. The officer watched helplessly as the driver squirmed through the shattered windshield, glanced at Elton, waved once more, and disappeared up the bank and into the night.

Elton reached for his radio to call for help. The holder was empty, its contents dislodged. It was likely somewhere in the car.

He was only a few yards from the other SUV when he smelled the gasoline and heard the moans. The vehicle was upright, but the roof was crushed and every window was smashed. He reached the driver's side just as a blood-covered hand appeared and grabbed the steering wheel.

The inside of the vehicle was a sea of deflated air bags. He reached through the window and pushed them out of the way, exposing the twisted, slumping body of the driver.

Heather Anderson looked up at him, dazed and silent. The moaning was coming from the passenger side of the vehicle. There was just enough light for Elton to see the driver, quickly assess her condition, and open the door.

Locked. He reached through the window again, found the handle, and forced open the dented door. Heather collapsed into his arms. He carried her 30 feet from the SUV and laid her gently on some grass.

She looked up at him through half-opened eyelids.

"Gracie." The name was a painful whisper.

Elton stood and spun around, facing the SUV. In the distance, he saw blue flashing lights and then heard the wail of a siren.

Chad. He must have left his makeshift blockade and come to help. Thank heaven.

Elton hurried to the passenger side of the SUV. The interior was dark, but he could just make out the outline of another person slumped against the dash.

Smoke! A black, acrid cloud was pouring from under the vehicle, burning his mouth and nose and searing his eyes. Elton looked down at his feet and saw the faint reflection of sparkling lights from his own high beams.

Gasoline.

The tank had ruptured, spilling its contents onto the highway.

Elton reached inside and opened the passenger door. An explosion, followed by a burst of flame, and he was blown backward onto the shoulder. The back of the SUV was ablaze. Flames were licking at the open passenger door and the young woman within. Another explosion and then more smoke—black, thick vapors enveloping everything.

"Elton! Get away from there!" It was Chad's voice, strident and insistent, coming from somewhere in the murky darkness.

Elton was dazed, momentarily confused by the explosion. He scrambled to his feet and staggered toward the SUV. Somehow—he still doesn't remember those moments—Elton was able to pull the young woman out of the vehicle and to safety.

Another explosion, and the SUV was engulfed in a consuming blaze.

"Elton, you're on fire!"

Chad was standing by Elton's side, pulling off his own jacket. Elton looked down at his arms. Both shirtsleeves were aflame.

The smell of burning flesh. Elton, a disbelieving spectator now, watched as Chad smothered his burning forearms with the jacket.

And then the pain.

I stood there, not knowing what to say to Elton Jones.

Without another word, he rolled up both sleeves and showed me the burn scars.

"That was a tough night, Doc. One I'll never forget."

"What about the girl?" I asked. "Gracie?"

"Now, *that* was a miracle. She had some bruises and a few cuts from the broken glass, but nothing broken and no burns anywhere. She was mighty lucky."

"Lucky it was *you* there that night," I told him. "And what about the driver? The other girl?"

"She had a broken wrist, but that was it. Their parents drove down from Michigan the next day and took them home." He paused and buttoned up the shirtsleeve that wasn't ripped apart. "Nice folks. I still get a card from them every Christmas."

"And what happened to the driver of that Explorer?" Lori asked. "He didn't get away, did he?"

Elton chuckled. "Almost. Took till morning and three dogs to hunt him down. Got five miles away before they found him. Tony Winston was his name. Turns out the Explorer was stolen. He had just robbed a convenience store in Charlotte at gunpoint and made a wrong turn on the interstate. I think they threw away the key when they locked him up."

"Wow," Lori sighed. "Anything could have happened out there that night. Sounds like he didn't care."

"No, he didn't."

Elton picked up his notebook and took a few steps toward the door. I couldn't help but think of my own two teenage girls—it could have been one of them.

"Elton," I called out.

The officer turned and our eyes met.

"Thank you."

If sacrifice is not the theme of my life,
there's no sense telling the story.
CRAIG D. LOUNSBROUG

2

The Ghost

Well, Doc, how bad is it?"

James Winn was lying comfortably on the stretcher in Cardiac. I had his EKG and lab work in my hands and had just looked at his chest X-ray. I knew I wouldn't be able to hide anything from him even if I'd wanted to. He knew me too well.

"James, things have gotten worse."

He nodded, but the smile on his face didn't change, and his eyes remained locked on mine.

"Figured. It feels different tonight somehow. Sorta like things are beginning to slip away." His voice was quiet but unstrained, and there was no hint of sadness in his words.

"We'll get some things started and—"

He raised a hand to silence me. "Doc, we both know where this road of heart failure leads. I'm way down it, and there's not much of it left. Can my wife and kids come back now?"

"Sure. I'll go get them."

I looked once more at this man who had been my friend for more than 25 years. And once again I was struck by the fact that though he looked to be no older than 45, he had the body and the heart of a man who'd celebrated 75 birthdays. And now his heart was failing him.

"I'll be right back with them."

I first met James when I started working in the ER of Rock Hill General Hospital. He was an orthopedic tech and knew more about bones and joints than any specialist on staff—before or since. He'd seen it all, and it didn't take me long to appreciate his experience, wisdom, and desire to help a wet-behind-the-ears ER doc.

"Dr. Lesslie, may I have a word?"

One of the nurses and I were in Minor Trauma and were struggling mightily to relocate the displaced shoulder of a 25-year-old inebriated victim of a slip-and-fall down three steps. I had decided on the Hippocratic technique, employing a hospital sheet in his armpit, anchored by my red-faced and sweating assistant on the other side of the stretcher. I was red-faced and sweating as well, and pulling as hard as I could on the young man's arm. There had been the occasional moan but not the welcome *clunk* of a dislocated shoulder sliding back into place.

"What?" I looked up into the face of James Winn, one of our orthotechs. He had duties throughout the hospital, and I hadn't called for his help. "We're fine here. Just give me another minute or so."

Another moan drifted up from the stretcher. The nurse grunted and then tried unsuccessfully to blow a wet tangle of hair from her forehead and out of her eyes.

"Just a word," he persisted.

I needed a break and nodded at the nurse. She immediately dropped the ends of the sheet and slumped into a nearby chair.

"Just an anterior dislocation, right?" James glanced at the somnolent patient. "Nothing broken?"

"That's right. As you can see, he's not very big or muscular, so I don't know why it hasn't popped back in."

"Sometimes these things can be tricky." He moved closer to the patient and placed a hand on the injured shoulder. "And sometimes there can be a little trick to getting them back into place."

James then proceeded to explain a simple maneuver that he thought might work. "Seen it happen a lot," he explained. "And you don't need someone pulling on the other side."

The nurse let out a sigh of relief, wiped her damp forehead, and slumped further into her chair.

I stepped closer to the stretcher and, following James's direction, firmly grabbed the young man's shoulder with one hand and his elbow with the other. "Like this?"

James nodded and folded his arms across his chest.

I followed his instructions, gently maneuvering the man's elbow and arm. *Clunk.*

"Oww!" It was a faint objection, and then our patient was asleep again. His shoulder was back in place, and when he was finally able to stand up and walk, he would be able to go home.

"Good work, Dr. Lesslie," the nurse said, slowly standing and smoothing the front of her dress.

I turned to thank James, but he was gone.

I began to understand that night why he was called "the ghost." He would appear out of nowhere at the very moment you needed him. And just as quickly, once he had helped you through some orthopedic difficulty, he would be gone. Like a ghost.

But there was something else going on with James. Something that took me a while to figure out.

When he was not a ghost—not suddenly appearing and disappearing—I'd see him standing with a few people, clearly the focus of their attention. He would listen to someone, nod his head, and then speak a few words. That was all. He had an audience, and with that audience he had a presence. His audience came in all shapes and sizes—young people, older people, med-techs, housekeepers, surgeons in their wrinkled scrubs...it didn't matter. People sought out James Winn for something, and after a while, my curiosity could stand it no longer. So I went to the source of all knowledge and all things political in the hospital—Virginia Granger, our ER head nurse.

"Do you understand what's going on with James Winn?" It was an early Wednesday morning, and I had just observed one of James's gatherings in the back of the ER. Two med-techs and one of the kitchen staff, all huddled around the ortho-tech. As I had walked past the group, I thought I heard one of the women say, "Preach on, James."

Virginia chuckled and pursed her lips.

"Took me a while to figure that one out too. James was here when my husband and I moved to Rock Hill, and he was a fixture in the hospital. As you've learned by now, he's an amazing ortho-tech—the best I've ever been around. But those people aren't seeking his advice for a backache or sore hip. They want his advice on other things—personal things. That man has endured a lot and possesses a lot of wisdom. And he possesses a spiritual wisdom that is quiet and unassuming but rock solid. He has the unusual ability…well, let's just say that if he gets to know you and you become friends, and he finds out you don't go to church and haven't been baptized…well, you'd better learn how to swim."

I glanced down the hallway and rubbed my chin.

"So when he's huddled up with people, he's sharing his life story, his spiritual walk. He's sharing the gospel."

Virginia nodded. "Might be. But more likely he's trying to help them with some personal problem. Could be a family member in trouble or a marriage on the rocks. Something like that. People around here trust him, and they trust what he has to say. That's a rare thing."

"Looks like it keeps him pretty busy."

She chuckled again. "Why do you think we call him the ghost? People would take all his time if they could. He probably needs to hang out a shingle somewhere and have his own counseling practice, but he loves what he does here. And he especially loves breaking in young ER doctors." She peered over the top of her black horn-rimmed glasses. "And how's that coming? Doing better with dislocated shoulders?"

My face flushed. She knew more about what was going on than I wanted her to.

"I'm doing just fine, thank you."

A few weeks later, our roles were reversed, and this time James Winn needed my help. Virginia had seen him standing in the doorway of the Orthopedic room, staring at the floor and rubbing his chest.

"Dr. Lesslie, I'm going to get James into Cardiac, and I want you to take a look at him."

It wasn't a request. I tossed the finished chart of room 3 into the discharge basket and headed toward the Cardiac room.

A few minutes later, James was in a gown and recumbent on the stretcher. Virginia stood at his side, arms folded rigidly across her chest.

"Tell me about this chest pain, James. When did it start?"

He was having a heart attack—the first of at least four. He tried to stay fit, walked everywhere he could, kept his blood pressure under control, and never smoked. He just couldn't overcome his genes. His father had died at 42 and his brother at 50.

Within 45 minutes, he had his "clot-buster" and was being wheeled to the cath lab. Three stents later, he was in the CCU and doing well.

I visited him upstairs the next morning. Returning to the ER, I was greeted by a waiting Virginia Granger.

"Well, how is he?"

I stood beside her and leaned against the counter of the nurses' station. "He's fine, and his cardiologist thinks he should do well. No evidence of any significant damage to his heart muscle, so that's good. I'm glad you convinced him to get checked out. I'm afraid to think what would have happened had he just ignored it and kept on working. Or gone home and gotten into trouble there."

"Didn't take much convincing him. James knew something was going on, and he knew he needed help. Glad to hear he's on the mend."

I shook my head and sighed. "If only he can get some rest up there. When I walked into the CCU, there were three or four people standing around his bed. They weren't staff from the unit, but from all over the hospital. And I think one was his preacher. He was asking James for his advice about something that was going on at church."

"Well, I suppose he's a captive now," Virginia chuckled. "But that will do him good, I think. He enjoys helping people, and he takes it seriously."

James *was* on the mend, and for a couple of years he had no cardiac problems. But then he had his second attack. One of the stents blocked off, and the muscle that it supplied died. His heart was a little weaker, but once again he recovered.

It was the third myocardial infarction that tipped the balance. It left too much damage, and he was on the slippery slope of heart failure. He understood the process and did everything he could to give himself the best chance to live as long and as well as he was able. But he had no cardiac reserve, and anything that taxed him—a simple infection, unexpected exertion, too much hidden salt in his diet—could flip the scales, and he would find himself short of breath and weak. This happened at least half a dozen times, and each time we were able to right the scales and get him stabilized. But each time it became more difficult. We knew—as did James—that it was only a matter of time before we wouldn't be able to help him.

Yet he continued to work as much as he could, pacing himself and working only partial shifts. His presence in the hospital and especially the ER was important. No, it was cherished. Those of us who knew him well understood how rare and valuable those moments were, and how much we needed his clinical wisdom. But more than that, we needed his spiritual guidance and insight. Knowing that we would have him for only a little longer made those times even more precious. For me, one of those moments happened at two in the morning, the day before Thanksgiving.

The only two patients in the department—a young couple suffering from restaurant-chain-induced food poisoning—were resting quietly in the observation room, plugged into IVs and enjoying a medication-induced sleep.

James had strolled into the department, checking to see if we had any orthopedic cases that might need his help. We had experienced an unseasonal ice storm a few days earlier, with the typical slips, falls, and fractures. But at the moment, we had no orthopedic injuries. He walked behind the nurses' station and sat down beside Amy Connors, the unit secretary. Jeff Ryan was the nurse in triage. The waiting room was empty, and Jeff stood leaning against the counter. I sat in a chair across from him.

I glanced around the group and stifled a chuckle. Here was James once again, surrounded by friends waiting on some word of wisdom, some pithy pearl.

But the talk was about the new hospital administrator, and then it was a comparison between the culinary virtues of a store-bought turkey versus a wild one. James knew how to cook, and if the conversation drifted to Thanksgiving recipes, I knew Jeff and I would be out of there.

It didn't. Instead, Amy tossed a small bombshell.

One of her best friends and high school classmates was in the final throes of a painful and damaging divorce. Any divorce is heartbreaking, but the past few months had taken a terrible toll on her friend's emotional and physical health.

"She's in real trouble," Amy told us. "And I'm afraid she might do something to herself. If she didn't have two small children, I'd really be worried. But she's a great mother and would never do anything that might hurt them."

We were silent for a moment, pondering this all-too-common crisis.

"She just doesn't know where it came from," Amy said quietly. "Never had any warning or saw any signs of trouble. Her husband claims there's no other woman, and she believes him."

Jeff cleared his throat and shifted in his chair. I glanced at him with eyes squinted.

Another moment of silence, and then James began to speak. We all looked at him and leaned a little closer.

"Well, this is what I've observed about relationships," he began.

"Doesn't matter whether it's a husband and wife, mother and daughter, brother and sister. They're all the same in one regard—every one of them is like one of the bones in your body."

James was an orthopedic technician and had spent his working years with bones and joints and ligaments. Yet my mind was stretching unsuccessfully to get itself around this unexpected analogy. I waited.

"Yep, just like a bone. In order for a bone—or a relationship—to be healthy, it takes attention. Proper care. With a bone, that means a healthy diet, calcium, exercise, all that stuff. With people, it takes *time*—that's real important—and listening. And mainly caring. You've got to put that other person in front of your own wants and needs, or it's not going to work. Things go wrong, just like with a bone. Take a stress fracture, for instance. Wear and tear, like too much walking on a hard surface, can weaken a bone. It starts to crack a little. And though you might not be able to see it on an X-ray, it's happening. Painful, maybe swollen, and getting weaker. If something's not done about it, it will eventually get worse and finally snap. Then you see it, and it's a full-fledged fracture.

"Now, sometimes you just have a routine run-of-the-mill fracture, like when someone falls and breaks their wrist. It's painful and demands immediate attention. You know something's wrong and that it has to be fixed. You're going to need help, like a good ortho-tech."

He paused and winked at us. "Or in the case of a relationship gone bad, it might be a good friend or a parent. But whichever, it needs fixin'. With the right treatment, splinting, and rest, that fracture will heal and get back to normal. But if it's neglected, you can end up with a leg or arm that's twisted and painful and always a problem. You know, sometimes that treatment can be painful. That fracture might require some twistin' and pullin' to get it back into place. And that can hurt."

"Just like a marriage," Amy interjected. "That makes a lot of sense—the stress fracture part. Sort of sneaks up on you, and then you've got real problems."

"You've got to pay attention," James continued. "Unless you just don't care. Sometimes that happens too. We've all seen people who've neglected their feet or ankles or knees. Hard to imagine how they get around, and hard to imagine why they haven't gotten help. After a while, it's just too late. Nothing that even the best orthopedic surgeon can do to help. Just too late."

I looked at Jeff and Amy, both staring silently at the tiled floor, each lost in their own thoughts. I wondered if James's words had struck an uncomfortable chord with them—as uncomfortable as the one he had struck within me.

James slapped his knees, blew out a long breath, then stood. "Anyway, the good news is that if you pay attention and do the right things, you can take care of your bones. And take care of the people you love."

"Preach on, James." Jeff nodded at his friend.

There it was again—that phrase. And at that moment, I knew. There was nothing serendipitous about these sessions with James or with the advice and wisdom he was dispensing. He was planting seeds—planting them with us now, just as he did throughout the hospital and throughout his life.

James Winn walked around the nurses' station and was gone. The ghost.

And now he was in the Cardiac room for the final time. His heart was giving out, and there was nothing I could do—nothing anyone could do. He knew it and was at peace.

"I think the whole family and then some must be in there." Amy nodded toward the Cardiac room. She had gone out to the waiting room and brought back James's family members. "Strange though. I didn't see a single tear."

I slowly pushed the door open and stuck my head into Cardiac, checking to be sure I wouldn't be banging into someone.

"Come on in, Dr. Lesslie." It was James's wife, Pearl. She was standing at the head of the stretcher, her hand resting gently on her husband's shoulder.

A crowd of 25 or 30 people surrounded the couple. It seemed each was trying to get as close to this dying man as possible. Yet Amy was right. There was not a tear in the room, only smiling faces. Almost joyful.

But why should that surprise me? James had lived a full life and had been a blessing to many—especially those now gathered around him. I knew the words of wisdom and kindness he had spoken to us here in the ER and throughout the hospital. I could only imagine the comfort his family had drawn from him through the years. The looks on their faces reflected that comfort and their love for this man.

"You see, Doc, this is what it all comes down to, isn't it?" His breath was coming harder now, but his voice was still firm and strong. "It's all about the people in your life, those that the Lord has placed around you. Ya got to be thankful. Always thankful."

An hour later, the ghost was gone.

Preach on, James. Preach on.

Have you had a kindness shown?
Pass it on, pass it on!
'Twas not given for thee alone,
Pass it on, pass it on!
Let it travel down the years,
Let it wipe another's tears,
Till in heaven the deed appears,
Pass it on, pass it on!

HENRY BURTON

3

The Widow-Maker

Okay, boys, what are the two things you have to remember if you're going to be a member of my crew?"

Captain Shep Stevens sat at the head of the kitchen table of Fire House 2. His team surrounded him: Engineer Roddy Langston, Firefighter 2 Bernie Tolbert, Firefighter Troy Adams, and Firefighter Lanny Woods. It was a Tuesday, and they had just finished their lunch—a meal prepared by Langston. Beef stew—his specialty.

"Rule number one," Woods offered. "Always leave the exhaust fan on in the bathroom."

The group laughed—everyone except Shep.

"Once again, what are the two things?" he repeated. "Whatever happens in the fire house—"

On cue, the four men recited, "Stays in the fire house."

"That's exactly right." Shep nodded at his engineer. "Isn't it, Roddy?"

Langston smiled and squirmed in his chair. "That's right, sir!" he snapped in military fashion.

His crewmates chuckled, remembering his initiation into this special group years earlier. For the most part, it had been innocent enough—nothing you couldn't tell your Sunday school teacher about. But there was that one visit to the ER with second-degree burns on his buttocks. Who would have thought that Texas Pete, the potent and popular hot sauce, could cause that kind of burn? But then, who in their right mind would pour a quart of it down the back of an unsuspecting initiate, causing it to settle in his pants and underwear? Roddy recovered, but the

ER doc didn't buy his story of backing into a hot oven. Nor did Chief Pritchard.

But, what happens in the fire house…

"And what's the other thing?" Shep persisted. "The most important?"

Troy raised his hand. "You've always told us that if we ever need to get out of a burning building or any other situation, all we have to do is tell you. No questions asked."

The group was silent, and Shep studied their faces.

"That's right." His voice was serious, his words measured. "If you ever need to leave or get out, tell me. That's all you need to do."

Silence again and nodding heads.

"Captain Stevens, I have a question."

"Fire away, Will. But call me Shep."

Stevens and trainee Will Gaston were alone in the equipment room.

"Okay…Shep. I'm confused about the different gas detectors we use—the ones attached to our masks. When do we pay attention to them, and when one lights up, what are we supposed to do?"

Stevens was checking his self-contained breathing apparatus—an SCBA. Its name described its function. It was a mask and hood that completely enclosed a firefighter's head and upper chest. The SCBA included a source of oxygen and had to fit tightly, ensuring that no smoke or gases entered the hood. It was heavy, but it was the safest and securest type of protective breathing equipment. The key was that it had to fit tightly—hence the crew's frequent inspection of this important and lifesaving gear.

The trainee continued. "I know about cyanide gas and how it can kill you in seconds. But how often do you really come into contact with it?"

Shep stopped what he was doing and looked at the 20-year-old. "In just about every house fire we respond to," he told him. "Keep in mind that everything that burns gives off different gases. That goes for paper and wood, but when furniture and upholstery burn, you can be sure there's cyanide being produced. Just about any kind of plastic will do it too. That's why we wear these SCBAs. With a house fire, you have to assume there's furniture or rugs on fire and that there's some level of cyanide present. And you're right about it killing you in just seconds."

He turned back to his equipment, studying each connection and tubing.

"That doesn't scare you, Captain? I mean…Shep?"

"Sure it scares me," Shep answered without stopping his inspections. "It's part of what we have to deal with. Cyanide and carbon monoxide—that's the dangerous one. Can't see it, can't smell it, and it slips up on you. Will, keep that in mind. *Every* fire you go to is making carbon monoxide. It's not as quick as cyanide, but when it gets you, you're just as dead."

Will stared at the floor, rubbing his chin.

He looked up at Shep. "In one of our classes, the instructor was talking about carbon monoxide and how dangerous it can be. He told us that someone in your crew had gotten into trouble with it a few years ago. Almost died."

Shep froze, and his mind flashed back to that February day, five years earlier.

It was supposed to be a routine call—if any call for a house fire could be routine. A small, single dwelling. No one inside. Easy access to a fire hydrant. Routine.

Not.

From the moment his engine company arrived at the scene, Shep's crew had trouble. The fire hydrant was indeed close to the burning house, but it was blocked by three pickup trucks, their drivers nowhere to be found.

The single dwelling was a two-story nightmare. It was surrounded by large, overhanging oaks on three sides, two of which were on fire. A ladder truck was on the way, but it was going to be difficult to find a good place to park it and get a ladder near the burning structure.

The house had a big, red, No Trespassing sign posted on the front door, but a neighbor had run up to Shep and told him a migrant family had been living there for the past four or five weeks.

So much for routine.

Shep gave his crew their orders and told them about the possibility of people being inside. Troy was standing near a large oak tree—one of the few that wasn't on fire. Huddled on the ground in front of him were a young man, a young woman, and two small children.

"Captain, do you speak Spanish?" he called out.

Shep hurried over to the group. Roddy and Lanny had found someone with keys to one of the pickup trucks. They had moved it and were attaching a fire hose to the hydrant.

After a few broken phrases, much pointing, and the nodding of several heads, Shep turned to Troy. "Another man and two kids took off a few minutes ago. Didn't want to be here when the police arrived." He turned to Roddy, Bernie, and Troy. "Come on with that hose! Let's go!"

The five firefighters stormed the front door, pulling the three-inch hose along with them. Somewhere in the distance a familiar siren announced the approach of the ladder truck. They would soon be getting some help.

Each of the men wore his SCBA—cumbersome but potentially life-saving. They didn't know what might be in the house and what they would be exposed to.

The front door was cracked open, and the crew burst into the living room. Shep paused, his team stopping behind him. There were only pockets of flames in this small space, but it wouldn't be long. The ceiling was smoking and beginning to sag—indications of an upstairs inferno.

Shep pointed to a room to their left. An old TV stood on a wooden table along one wall, faced by a small, upholstered sofa—some sort of worn and faded Naugahyde. It was smoking, steaming from the heat.

He pointed to his mask and nodded. His crew understood his signal, and they understood the potential for cyanide gas.

Shep took a deep breath. Somebody had to go upstairs, and the remainder of the downstairs had to be checked. The man outside thought the house was empty, but Shep knew better than to make assumptions.

He spoke into the voice amplifier in his hood. "Troy, Lanny, Bernie—you guys make sure these rooms are clear. Roddy, come with me."

The crew separated, and Shep and the engineer headed up the narrow stairs.

The upstairs landing opened onto three small bedrooms and a bath. The bedroom to the left was completely engulfed in flames—right over the living room. It would only be minutes before that part of the house collapsed.

The bathroom in front of them was empty, leaving the two bedrooms on their right to be searched.

Roddy heard it first. He cocked his head, straining his ears, trying to identify the location of what had sounded like the cry of a small child.

There it was again, and Shep heard it this time.

He pointed to one of the bedrooms and motioned for Roddy to stay where he was. Flames were lapping at the doorway, and smoke clouded their visibility. Shep hurried into the room, scanning the four corners. Nothing.

A twin bed was pushed up against the far wall, its gray blanket on fire. The window over the bed burst into a thousand small shards of glass, exploding from the heat. Another cry—more of a scream this time—came from under the bed. Shep reached down, grabbed the edge of the bed, and threw it to one side. A three-year-old boy lay curled at the firefighter's feet, his large brown eyes looking up into the Shep's plastic face mask.

The boy reached out his arms. Shep scooped him up and raced for the doorway. Another window exploded somewhere upstairs, and a couple of burning floor joists gave up and fell into the living room. They were running out of time.

Roddy had remained on the landing as instructed. As Shep walked up with the boy, the engineer pointed to the remaining bedroom, then to himself.

"Okay, but hurry up!" Shep told him.

Roddy turned just as the boy in Shep's arms reached out for him, grabbing part of his hood and oxygen tubing. There was a hiss, and some unseen part of the SCBA fell on the wooden floor. Roddy's hood was compromised. He stared at Shep for a split second and then glanced downstairs. The burning sofa.

Shep's cyanide monitor had remained silent, reassuring the captain. Loud beeping, and Shep's body tensed. The carbon monoxide monitor was issuing its warning.

Roddy saw it too, and his eyes widened.

"You need to leave? Do you need to get out?" Shep searched his friend's face for an answer. They *both* needed to get out, but there was one more room to search.

Shep moved toward the engineer and lifted the child toward him.

"No, I got this." Roddy spun around, and with a couple of long strides, he was in the bedroom, standing in the middle of billowing smoke. He coughed a few times and then reached out for the nearest wall. He could see only a foot or two in front of him, and searching this room would have to be done by hand.

Shep bolted down the stairway with the boy. They passed through the now-flaming living room and out into the yard.

A crowd had gathered—curious onlookers. A few cheers and a smattering of applause greeted the firefighter and his wide-eyed cargo.

Crew members from the ladder truck ran up. Shep lowered the boy to the ground and turned to the firefighters. Something tugged at his right leg and he looked down. The child was grabbing Shep's pant leg and wasn't about to let go.

"What's going on, Captain?" one of the men asked.

Shep told him what he knew and had seen in the house, and then he told him about Roddy.

He should be out here by now!

Shep turned around and faced the house. Every window was broken and filled with licking flames. They all could feel the intense heat of this fire, even from 60 feet away.

He took a step toward the house and froze. Bursting through the dense smoke filling the front doorway, Roddy appeared, carrying another young child—this one a two-year-old girl. The engineer had wrapped a small towel around her face and held her close to his chest.

Troy and Lanny ran up to them, and Lanny grabbed the little girl and took the towel from her face. She coughed once, looked around, and settled back in his arms.

Roddy ripped off his hood and took in long, deep breaths.

"You okay?" Shep asked him.

His crewmates stood beside the engineer, studying his face and eyes. "I'm okay."

The house burned to the ground—too far gone to salvage. The two children were reunited with their runaway uncle, but only briefly. The state's department of social services intervened, and the brother and sister were placed with a young and caring couple.

Nothing routine about this house fire.

And there would be another not-so-routine fire that Shep's crew responded to three weeks later.

The call came in as an apartment fire, and within minutes, it was a multiple alarm. Every available engine was on its way to a complex on Grady Avenue. Three floors high, 60 units…a nightmare.

Shep and his crew were the third engine to arrive. They were assigned to a "heavy rescue" truck—a six-man crew whose main function was to rescue other firefighters. When they pulled into the crowded parking area, Chief Pritchard was already there, directing his teams as they arrived.

"Shep, I know you're on rescue, but this thing is getting out of control, and we don't know if anyone is still in the building. I need your crew to grab a hose and head for the third floor."

Pritchard pointed at the top level of the sprawling complex. Smoke was billowing from the entire structure, and flames were leaping from the roof in the center of the L-shaped building. Right where Pritchard was pointing.

"Gotcha, Chief."

Shep turned to his crew. "Troy, Lanny—get that hose connected to a hydrant and let's get up there." He glanced at Roddy Langston and winked. "And make sure your equipment's airtight."

It took all six of the men to lift the six-inch hose and carry it into the main entrance. A small lobby opened to a glassed ceiling, with a wide stairway opening onto the second and third levels. Hallways extended right and left from each landing. Two elevators stood open in the back of the tiled space—locked and useless.

"Let's go!" Shep hollered through his SCBA hood.

Troy took the lead and headed up the stairs. Smoke and flames were everywhere, and the giant hose sprayed a steady stream of water ahead of them and down each hallway they passed. Off somewhere to their left, they heard an explosion, but they didn't stop or even turn their heads.

This was hard work—hot and heavy. Each of these men had passed strenuous fitness exams, but nothing ever really prepared someone for this kind of exertion. Shep was sweating and gasping for breath as Troy reached the third-floor landing just ahead of him.

The younger firefighter looked at his captain, his eyebrows raised.

Shep was second in line on the hose. He took one hand off just long enough to point to the hallway to their right. Troy nodded and turned in that direction.

Something snagged the hose, and their progress came to a sudden stop. Water was still flowing, so it wasn't kinked. Roddy was right behind Shep, and he gave a big tug, grunting as he did so. Shep and Troy did the same thing. The hose broke loose, and they were moving again. Shep had reached the hallway when he felt a forceful tap on his shoulder. He turned around and looked into the terrified face of Roddy Langston. He was pale, and his lips were blue.

"Shep, I gotta get out of here. I've got to leave."

Shep studied his face. "What's the matter, Roddy?"

"I gotta go."

Shep grabbed Troy's shoulder, and the firefighter turned around.

"I'm taking Roddy outside," he told him. "Keep the crew here, and I'll send up some help."

Roddy had released the hose and was standing in the middle of the landing. One knee buckled, and Shep grabbed him.

Somehow they made it down the steps and through the lobby. Once outside, Shep looked around, saw two paramedics, and hollered at them.

"Hey, I need some help over here!"

He pulled off Roddy's hood and helped the engineer to the ground. "What's the matter?" one of the paramedics asked him.

Roddy's eyes were closed. He shook his head and put a hand on his chest.

The paramedic knelt beside Roddy, looked up at his partner, and said, "Get the monitor and the medical box."

They worked quickly and smoothly, and within a few minutes the paper of a 12-lead EKG strip was flowing out of the cardiac monitor.

The lead paramedic held the strip in his hands, shook his head, and held it up for Shep to see. Shep wasn't a cardiologist, but he had seen enough EKGs and rhythm strips to know this wasn't good. At age 42, Roddy Langston was in the middle of a heart attack.

Shep's wife, Cathy, was a nurse in the ICU at Memorial Hospital. It was a simple matter for her to get Shep and Troy into the small viewing area in the cath lab. It was elevated with large windows, overlooking the treatment table and multiple monitors below. It wasn't for friends or family but was used for teaching residents and observing difficult cases.

Roddy was lying on the table, flat on his back, his eyes closed. His color was still terrible, which was one of the things that got the attention of the ER doctor. Eight minutes from door to cath lab—pretty good. But it had to be if they were going to save this firefighter.

One of the staff cardiologists happened to be in the ER and had looked at Roddy's EKG. "Get the crew ready," he told the ER secretary. "Let's go."

Roddy's right groin was stained with Betadine, and a large-bore needle protruded from his skin. The cardiologist—masked and wearing bifocals—threaded a pliable catheter through the needle and up toward Roddy's heart. Several monitors flashed on, and Shep and Troy watched everything.

The catheter tip snaked into view, passing through a large blood vessel and into the right side of the heart. Slower progress now, and they watched as the tip was positioned near the mouths of the coronary arteries—the vessels that feed the heart muscle itself.

The cardiologist paused, straightened, and glued his eyes to one of the screens. He nodded, and a bright flash of contrast liquid exited the tip of the catheter and entered one of the coronary vessels. Stark white against the dark screen, it was easy to see its progress through Roddy's vessels. Then the column of contrast and blood stopped. It was the clot—the cause of his heart attack. Nothing was flowing beyond it, and the muscle this vessel supplied was dying.

"The widow-maker," Shep whispered. It was the main vessel supplying the heart, and when it was clotted off, bad things happened and widows were made.

Troy looked at his captain. "What now? What can they do?"

The two men watched as the cardiologist slowly advanced the catheter tip into the middle of the clot.

"He's going to try to open it up with a balloon," Shep said quietly.

The cardiologist held a device in his hands that connected to the catheter. Without taking his eyes off the screen, he slowly inflated the balloon located just behind the tip of the catheter. If the clot was still soft, it could be compressed against the vessel wall, and life-giving blood would flow to the threatened heart muscle. If not…

One of the nurses called out, "60 over 40." Roddy's blood pressure was continuing to fall and was now at a dangerous level. The cardiologist glanced down at him and back up at the monitor.

Every eye in the room stared at the screen and the tip of the catheter.

"Forty over nothing."

Shep and Troy stood frozen—barely breathing—and stared helplessly at the drama unfolding in the room beneath them.

A murmur from below, and they watched as a small trickle of contrast made its way through the clot and beyond the catheter tip. Then a whole column of blood flooded the vessels beyond the now-open clot, bathing the starving muscle with oxygen.

Troy grabbed Shep's arm and squeezed it with all his might.

The two firefighters couldn't help themselves as they let out a loud yelp.

Roddy's eyes opened, and his head turned to the observation platform. He slowly raised his right hand, smiled, and gave them a thumbs-up.

They returned his salute but then froze again. The cardiologist's dark, piercing eyes were staring at them over the tops of his glasses.

"One hundred over 60," the nurse reported.

The cardiologist didn't flinch—just kept his eyes focused on the two firefighters. Slowly he raised his hand, clenched his fist…and pointed his thumb toward the ceiling.

Four months later, Roddy was back at work.

"Just a crazy thing," he told his crew members. "They can't explain why it happened, but it did. No heart damage though. I feel great, and they think I'm going to be fine."

A loud blast on the alarm horn. "Engine 2, respond to a house fire—412 East Green Street."

Shep looked around at his crew.

"Let's go!"

A band of brothers.

4

In the Nick of Time

*As long as the world is turning and spinning, we're
gonna be dizzy and we're gonna make mistakes.*

MEL BROOKS

Denton Roberts slumped into an empty chair at the nurses' station and propped his boots on the desk. Amy Connors turned her head in his direction and seemed about to say something, but she must have thought better of it. Denton and his partner had been running all day long, having just deposited a 25-year-old auto-accident victim in the Trauma room. The paramedic deserved a break.

"Nothing serious, Doc. A bruised knee from bangin' it into the dash, but seems okay. And a little left shoulder pain from his seat belt. Lungs and heart and everything are good. His mother insisted we bring him in by ambulance, so we did."

He continued writing on the young man's emergency medical services (EMS) record and exhaled a loud sigh.

"What a day. I think we set a record for the number of runs in 24 hours. Haven't been able to sit down, much less get something to eat."

I glanced at the clock above the medicine room doorway. A little after midnight. Maybe things would quiet down and he and his partner could catch a break.

"There might be something in the fridge back in the lounge," Amy volunteered. "One of the drug reps brought lunch in yesterday, and I think there were some ham sandwiches left over."

"That's all I need—food poisoning. A little salmonella would make the day absolutely perfect. Thanks, but no thanks."

Ronnie Greenly, Denton's partner, walked out of Trauma and over to the nurses' station. He propped his elbows on the countertop and leaned forward.

"I don't know how it could have been a worse day," he said to the group gathered in front of him. "We never stopped."

"Well, I know how it could have been worse," Amy chimed in. "What if Divine Savior was still open and you had to cover that as well?"

Ronnie slumped on the counter and shook his head.

What in the world made Amy think of Divine Savior? That long-gone brick building hadn't crossed my mind in years.

"You're right—it could have been worse," Ronnie agreed. "Thank heaven for small favors."

Divine Savior had been a small hospital in York, with only a few dozen beds and a 24-hour ER. Anybody who was really sick or injured usually drove the 12 or so miles to Rock Hill General, but sometimes true emergencies wandered in if it was the closest ER and someone didn't know better. The emergency department physician coverage was often suspect, thus necessitating the county keeping an EMS unit in the building. If someone was really sick, they needed to be elsewhere, and quickly.

"Best thing that ever happened to York when it closed," Amy said. "I know a lot of people on that side of the county didn't want to see it go, but it was the best thing for everybody. There were some strange things going on in that ER—let alone upstairs. You know that, Denton. All too well. In fact, you saved my uncle one night over there, remember? Jackson Connors?"

Denton looked up from his charting and cocked his head at the unit secretary.

"Jackson Connors," he drawled, rubbing his chin. "Sounds familiar. Was he…yeah, I remember. New Year's Eve, if I'm correct."

"That's right." Amy smiled at the paramedic and nodded. "New Year's Eve, and Uncle Jackson will never forget it. You saved him, and just in the nick of time."

Denton flushed. "Don't know about all that, but I do remember that night."

Amy twisted in her seat and looked at me. "And you remember it too, Dr. Lesslie. You were on duty here when they brought him in."

I nodded. How could I forget?

An ice storm had pelted the area during that interholiday week. Four days after Christmas, the county ground to a halt. Roads were slick and impassable, power lines were down, and most people knew to stay put and in their homes.

But not everybody. Sleet and ice—much more so than snow—are an orthopedist's nightmare. Or blessing, depending on who's looking at it. Slips and falls, fractures and breaks—the ER is always busy when freezing precipitation pays us a visit. That's true for Rock Hill—and most of the southeast—with people of all ages venturing onto slick and shiny sidewalks and steps. It's also true when it comes to driving. You'd think that the part of the world that gave us NASCAR would also have produced better drivers. Hasn't happened yet.

It was New Year's Eve. Jackson Connors had ventured out after three days of being cooped up. Cabin fever, he had called it.

"We need some milk and bread and a couple of things," he told his wife, with one hand on the front doorknob. "Anything special you need?"

"You just be careful," she called from the kitchen. "We really don't need any of that stuff. You just need to get out, that's all."

"I'll be careful. Don't worry."

Jackson safely negotiated the mile and a half to the Winn Dixie, carefully picked his way back to the car, and made it home without incident. A few skids on Highway 161, but he kept it between the ditches and pulled into his driveway.

He didn't see the patch of black ice on the sidewalk, and that's what did him in. With both arms loaded with grocery bags clutched high on his chest, Jackson closed the passenger door with his hip. He took two steps toward the house, and in a split second was lying on his right side.

Spilled milk was puddling in front of him, and he was hurting. Right hip, right chest, and right shoulder. The shoulder was killing him. Sharp, piercing pain—unlike anything he had ever felt.

He was alone in the driveway, not sure whether he should try to move. But his wife would have no way of knowing he was lying just yards from her, freezing.

Jackson shifted his weight, testing his right hip with just a little pressure. It felt okay, and he tried to sit.

The pain in his right shoulder jolted him, and he couldn't suppress a loud moan. Something was wrong—broken. He didn't move and prayed for the pain to pass.

At least the hip seems okay. I can deal with a busted shoulder, but a fractured hip would mean something else.

A neighbor's dog barked, and Jackson glanced in its direction.

Baggins, the Smiths' golden retriever, stood at the edge of the property, staring at the prostrate man. The dog's tail wagged, shaking his entire body.

Another bark, more tail-wagging, and Jackson motioned him over. Baggins bounded through the ice-covered grass to his friend and started licking Jackson's face. The kisses were wet and sloppy, and Jackson knew it was time to get up and get inside where it was warm. And where he could call for an ambulance.

He knew what was coming and braced himself as best he could. Jackson planted his left hand on the sidewalk, shifted his legs underneath him, and slowly stood.

A pained cry shattered the afternoon quiet, and Baggins's ears drooped against the side of his head. The dog leaned into the man and looked up into his face.

"I'm okay, boy. Thanks for being here."

Jackson made it to the door, turned the doorknob, and slumped into the living room. Baggins followed and sat by the front door, his long, feathered tail sweeping gracefully across the hardwood floor.

"What in the world?" his wife asked, appearing from the direction of the kitchen. "Why are you…?"

She ran to her husband, put her arms around him, and helped him to the sofa.

"I need some help," he whispered. "Better call 911."

An hour later, Jackson Connors was lying on a stretcher in the ER of Divine Savior Hospital. The physician on duty—a moonlighting doctor from the Columbia area—had made a quick preliminary exam.

"I think your hip is fine, Mr. Connors," Dr. Bates told him. "Your right ribs are at least bruised. We'll get some X-rays of those areas in a while, but right now we need to get that shoulder back in place. It's dislocated, and once it's reduced, you'll feel a lot better. Let me get some help."

The ER doc turned and walked toward the nurses' station.

Jackson's wife laid a gentle hand on his uninjured shoulder. "Well, that's good news. At least your hip is fine. And once we get that shoulder fixed, you're going to feel a whole lot better."

"Don't count on it."

Jackson and his wife jerked their heads in the direction of the low, rumbling voice. It had come from behind the curtain to their left.

A sun-worn, gnarly hand appeared at the edge of the curtain and slowly pulled it back. Lying on a stretcher was a middle-aged man. His eyes moved from Jackson to his wife, and he shook his head.

"I've been here five hours, and nothin'. Somebody came and got some blood out of my arm and told me to pee in a urinal. The doctor said she'd be back with some reports, but that ain't happenin'. I'm about ready to put on my clothes and leave." He propped himself up on the stretcher and glanced around the space in his small cubicle. "If I could find them."

"Mr. Flinn, lie back down and stop bothering these people." One of the nurses had walked into Jackson's cubicle. She stopped at the head of his stretcher and closed his neighbor's curtain.

The disgruntled Mr. Flinn only harrumphed.

The nurse reached into a shelf on the stainless-steel rolling cart near the head of Jackson's stretcher. She picked up a hospital sheet and began to unfold it.

Ever observant, Jackson noticed the laundry imprint on one of the edges of the sheet.

"Greenville General Hospital," he said, pointing to the mark. "That sheet seems to get around."

The nurse paused and looked at the circular imprint. "You're right. Probably has. We get them from all over—as far away as a hospital in Virginia. I think we even had one in here last month from Florida. Seems like hospital sheets get around as much as a juicy rumor."

"Okay, let's see if we can get that shoulder back in place." Dr. Bates had stepped into the room and stood with her hands on her hips.

"Lucille," she addressed the nurse, "slide that sheet under Mr. Connors's right armpit and cinch it up tight."

Lucille complied, lifting Jackson's arm and eliciting a painful outcry. His wife winced and stepped forward.

"Please be careful," she told the nurse. "That shoulder is killing him."

Lucille cast a curt glance in her direction and proceeded to pull the sheet under Jackson's back and over his chest—anchoring it in his right armpit. She held both loose ends and pulled them tight, snugging the makeshift countertraction into position. She had done this before and knew what was coming next. She wrapped one of the loose ends around her expansive hips and prepared to brace against it—a trick one of the night-shift supervisors had taught her.

"Ready here," she told the ER doctor.

"Is this gonna hurt much?" Jackson asked, suspecting the answer.

"Only for a moment," Dr. Bates said. "Then you'll be fine."

"What about some pain medication first?" his wife asked.

The ER doc paused. Her eyebrows furrowed, and Mrs. Connors wondered if she might have forgotten something.

The look quickly passed, and she shook her head. "No, we'll have this shoulder back in place before any pain medicine would take effect." She was standing at the right side of the stretcher and reached out, taking

Jackson's wrist in her two hands. "I want you to try to relax and let us do the work. You might feel a little pressure or pulling."

The ER doc glanced up at Lucille and nodded. "Hold tight."

An earsplitting scream sliced through the room, and Mr. Flinn's curtain jerked open. Wide-eyed, he surveyed the scene in front of him.

Lucille—all 250 pounds of her—was leaning backward and pulling for all she was worth. The sheet was taut across Jackson's chest, creating a stable anchor against which the red-faced ER doc was pulling.

She was leaning backward as well, applying all her weight while huffing and puffing and straining, as if her intent was to separate Jackson Connors's arm from his body.

He was past screaming now and stared at the ceiling, his mouth open.

"I need to take a break," Lucille panted, sweat pouring down her puffy cheeks.

"Okay," the ER doc agreed. "Let's give it a minute."

She relaxed her grip on Jackson's wrist, and the man let out a relieved sigh.

"It's not back in place yet?" his wife asked the doctor. "You pulled on it a long time—surely it's all right now."

"Not yet, but I think it's just about ready to go back in. You have to fatigue those shoulder muscles—get them to relax—and the head of the humerus just slips back in. Your husband is strong, so it's just taking a little longer than usual."

"What about something for pain now?" Mrs. Connors persisted. "This is really hurting him."

Bates looked at her wristwatch and didn't respond.

"You ready, Lucille?"

The nurse had been slouching on one of the rolling stools. She nodded without a word and slowly got to her feet. When she had the sheet wrapped around her again and both ends firmly in hand, she said, "Ready on this end."

"Let's go then."

They repeated the process—Lucille applying as much pressure as she could to Jackson's armpit, the ER doc yanking his wrist and leaning back—almost falling over—and Jackson grimacing and moaning. This went on for another ten minutes, with no relocation of the man's shoulder. They took another break, the ER doc rebuffed another request for pain medication, and then went at it again.

Jackson's wife was at her wit's end. Without a word, she slipped out of the cubicle and walked over to the nurses' station. The unit secretary was reading the latest issue of *People* magazine and didn't look up when Jenny Connors asked if she could use one of the telephones. The secretary pointed to the end of the counter and turned a page.

Mrs. Connors picked up the phone, glanced around the department, tucked her head, and dialed 911.

"What's your emergency?" a tired, matter-of-fact voice answered.

"I'm in the ER and I need an ambulance."

A pause on the other end of the line, and Mrs. Connors felt foolish. She was about to say something when the dispatcher asked, "Are you at Divine Savior?"

How did she know? What had...

"Yes, I'm in the ER at Divine Savior Hospital and my husband needs an ambulance right now."

She sneaked a peek at the unit secretary, whose face was still buried in her magazine, still oblivious.

"Just stay where you are, ma'am. It'll just be a minute."

The receiver clicked, and Jackson's wife stared at the phone.

Somewhere down a long hallway, a phone rang. A moment later, the sound of footsteps approached the nurses' station, and Denton Roberts was standing in front of Jenny Connors.

"Do you need an ambulance, ma'am?" He studied the woman's face and then looked beyond her to the treatment areas. Lucille and the ER doctor were still at work, still pulling on the arm and trunk of Jackson Connors.

"Yes. Please, come with me."

She turned and hurried in the direction of her husband's fatigued moans.

It was no small feat, convincing the ER doctor that her husband needed to be taken to Rock Hill General. Mrs. Connors had made the initial request, but Dr. Bates rejected the idea, telling her that she had almost completed her evaluation and treatment of Jackson and that another hospital and another doctor would have nothing to offer. It took Denton Roberts pushing his stretcher beside that of Jackson Connors and lifting the injured man to drive home the point.

"We'll be transporting him to Rock Hill at the patient's request," he had said flatly.

The ER doctor glowered at him briefly, picked up Jackson's chart, and huffed toward the nurses' station. She stopped and spun around. "Fine. But it's against my medical advice."

Lucille, thankful for the release, headed outside to smoke a cigarette.

"Tell whoever's on duty in the ER over there that we didn't have time to make any X-rays," Bates told Denton. She looked toward Jenny Connors. "We can still get those, if you want."

"No, we're ready to go now," Mrs. Connors said.

"The sooner the better," Jackson muttered.

"What was that?" The doctor's head jerked in his direction.

"I said, 'Thanks for all your help,'" Jackson lied.

Denton drove as gently as he could, trying to avoid the many potholes scattered on Highway 161. The slightest bounce brought a pained moan from the back of the ambulance. Jackson's shoulder was killing him.

When they arrived in the ER, Amy Connors was waiting for them. Jackson's wife had called and told her they were on the way. She was standing beside me at the nurses' station as Denton and his partner pushed Jackson's stretcher down the hallway to the Ortho room.

"I'll never forget the look on your face when you examined him, Dr. Lesslie." Amy shook her head, unsmiling. "You didn't say anything, but I knew something was wrong."

"You were right about that, Amy. When I felt his shoulder, I knew something was peculiar, and I wanted to see his X-rays."

"Your face turned red when Denton told you there were no X-rays. They hadn't done any at Divine Savior, and you were fit to be tied."

"Mad as fire was more like it," I agreed. "And when we took X-rays of his shoulder, I was livid."

"I remember you pointing at his shoulder joint and explaining it to Aunt Jenny and me," Amy said. "His shoulder joint was fine—perfectly in place. Never was dislocated. It was his AC joint that was the problem—that place on top of the shoulder where football players get injured."

"Worst AC separation I've ever seen." I held my right thumb and index finger an inch apart. "Just about this much separation. And every time that ER doc over at Divine Savior pulled on it, the separation got worse."

"Who knows?" Amy interjected. "If they had stayed at it a little longer, they might have pulled his arm off."

I chuckled. "Well, probably not. But I still wonder if he went in there with a simple AC strain—no separation—and left with a complete separation that took him to the OR."

I had called the ER doctor at Divine Savior that night, ready to blast her. Something stopped me though, and calmness prevailed. It was uncomfortable, but I realized I had been down my own share of wrong paths. I made the call and calmly explained the diagnosis and the treatment. "We all make mistakes, " I added. This had turned into a teachable moment—for her and for me.

"How's he doing now?" Denton leaned forward in his chair. "Having any residual problems with that shoulder?"

"No, he's fine. Good range of motion and everything. But it's like I said, Denton, you saved him that night. Just ask him—or ask Aunt Jenny. They'll tell you."

Just in the nick of time.

You must learn from the mistakes of others.
You can't possibly live long enough
to make them all yourself.

SAMUEL LEVENSON

5

Maybelle Jenkins

August 1977

The Special Care Nursery was a world of its own—bright lights, beeping monitors, intense and focused nurses and physicians, and tiny babies struggling to stay alive. And there was Maybelle Jenkins, rocking quietly in a corner of the room, cradling one of those tiny infants. She hummed softly, carefully adjusted the blanket wrapping her young charge, and studied the controlled frenzy of the large, open unit. She had been doing this for the past 20 years—an unassuming yet essential fixture of the old Greenville General Hospital.

I spent my first three months after graduating from medical school in the Special Care Nursery at the General, and I quickly got to know Maybelle. Her job was "to tend to the littlest ones," making sure they each had some caring physical contact each day. Some of the newborns weren't able to leave the confines of their incubators, having to be kept warm and closely monitored. Most had several IVs going as well as feeding tubes. But even these infants could be held and rocked for a while, and they needed to be. This was part of their therapy—part of our effort to keep them alive and to help them make it past this critical period of their new lives.

At first, I was skeptical about this holding and rocking business. I was all about the monitors and tubes and IVs. Those were the things I understood and could deal with. But Maybelle taught me about the rocking chairs in the corner of the room, next to the windows overlooking the tree-canopied neighborhoods surrounding the General.

Something important happened here, something I thought couldn't be tested or measured or monitored. But that something *could* be measured. These infants thrived, and they gained weight. That was how we often measured success in the nursery—not just keeping these little ones alive, but watching and making sure they were growing. That's where these rocking chairs—and Maybelle—made a big difference.

Many of our young patients had parents who couldn't spend much time away from home, their other children, or their jobs. And since these infants were frequently in the nursery for several months, any help was appreciated.

But not everyone could do this kind of thing. It required patience and love, and it required looking at it as a calling. The women who did this work weren't paid anything and did so out of a sense of concern for the critical infants. But most didn't stay with it for very long. The Special Care Nursery was a stressful place, with almost hourly emergencies sending a group of caregivers to the bed of a distressed child. Not every emergency had a good ending, and the loss of these little ones took its toll on all of us—maybe more so on the women who had invested so many hours rocking and cradling them.

But Maybelle stayed—more than two decades—even though she came to the nursery many mornings to find her assigned bassinet empty. Even then, she stayed.

And she watched. She quickly sized up the new residents that rotated through the unit and the new nurses who transferred in, thinking this was something they wanted to do. She could tell who really cared about her children, who was only marking time, and who had no clue what was going on in this place. She rocked and hummed and watched.

In 1977, I was one of those new residents, and Maybelle had her eye on me. I liked the pace and the intensity of the unit, and I liked working with these sick and tiny kids. When I had a moment, I would sit down next to Maybelle while she rocked one of our small bundles. We would talk for a while—actually, I would be the one talking. She listened and rocked and every once in a while nodded her head.

One day she did talk, and it surprised me. It was a Friday afternoon, and the nursery was relatively quiet after a busy week. Greenville General was the referral center for the upstate of South Carolina, and we were expecting a transfer from an outlying hospital. The information from the referring physician had not been very clear, and we weren't sure what to expect.

When the nursery doors opened and an EMS unit rolled their stretcher into the unit, Maybelle shook her head and muttered the name of the hospital emblazoned on one of the paramedic's jackets.

"Dr. Lesslie, there's no tellin' what they're sendin' you. You better be real careful and start from scratch with that child."

I didn't know it at that moment, but she was right.

The referring physician's report had been brief—a three-month-old male with listlessness, poor feeding, and constipation. No fever and no abnormal heart or lung problems. Not much to go on.

John Simmons, the third-year pediatric resident in the unit that afternoon, directed the arriving EMS personnel to an empty bassinet in the middle of the room. I stood behind his shoulder as they stopped beside the tiny bed and unlatched the cover of the plastic incubator. They had been using humidified oxygen, and the inside of the clear container was fogged. When one of our nurses carefully reached in and lifted the child, a troubling grunt issued from Simmons. He shook his head.

This was more than listless. The child had no muscle tone and flopped loosely in the nurse's hands. His color was a dusky gray, and his eyes were sunken and half-closed. We didn't have much time.

"His name is Cecil Flanders."

I looked up into the flushed face of the transfer nurse from the original hospital.

"Cecil," she repeated. "He's 14 weeks old." She picked up a clipboard from the stretcher and held it out to Simmons. "His mother brought him to our ER yesterday with complaints of eating poorly and sleeping all the time. The ER docs consulted the family practitioner on call for pediatrics, and he put him in the hospital. I think they tried to start an IV but couldn't—he's so small and everything. And when he didn't improve overnight, they decided to send him here."

Simmons and I both glanced at the clock on the wall in front of us. What had taken them so long? Their hospital was only an hour or so away. Why the delay?

A swarm of activity surrounded Cecil's bed. An IV was started, monitors attached, and lab and X-ray were called in. He was in trouble, and we all knew it.

"Any medical problems?" Simmons was examining the child now and didn't look up at the transfer nurse. "Normal pregnancy? Normal delivery?"

"No, everything had been fine," the nurse answered. "His mother was right behind us and should be here any minute. She'll know a lot more, but I think he's been fine up until the last day or two. She has two other children, and I think she did mention that one of them had done the same kind of thing. Outgrew it and—"

"Heart rate is 80 and his temp is low." One of the unit nurses cast a worried look at Simmons. "He didn't flinch at all when I checked his rectal temp."

A heart rate of 80 was dangerously low for a child this young, and a low core temperature could be due to several things—none of them good.

"What have we got here?"

Dr. Joel Lipsky, the new director of the Special Care Nursery, walked up to the bed. The transfer nurse moved out of his way and walked over to where the EMS personnel were securing their stretcher.

"This is our new admission?" He adjusted his glasses and reached for some exam gloves.

Joel Lipsky had been at the General for six months, fresh from completing his neonatology fellowship at Johns Hopkins in Baltimore. He was bright, tireless, and unburdened by a sense of humor. When it came to managing the unit, he was all business, and he expected the same from us. Morning and afternoon "rounds" were exercises in humility for those of us in his charge. If we knew the answer to his question concerning a particular child or problem, the odds were not very good at being able to answer the next one. Or the one after that. He challenged us, and the reference texts and journals in our small call room collected no dust. But we were learning, and the reputation of the unit had been enhanced since his arrival.

"Blood sugar?" Lipsky called out. "And what's his blood pressure?"

His examination of Cecil continued. Lab reports were returned, and a total-body X-ray hung on a view box a few steps away. No help with any of this. All of his blood chemistries were normal, and his X-ray was fine—no pneumonia or abnormal heart shape or size. His EKG was also normal except for the slow heart rate.

"Okay, staff, what do you think is going on with our young man?" Lipsky stepped back from the bedside, peeled off his gloves, and tossed them into a nearby trash can. "What do we need to be looking for?"

I cleared my throat and looked at John Simmons.

"Well…" John paused, rubbing his chin. "We need to think about the possibility of infection even though his white count is normal. Low heart rate and low temperature—those are concerns and would fit that picture."

"What about his heart?" Lipsky pried. "Are you satisfied with his EKG and X-ray? Could a cardiac problem cause these findings?" He looked at my name tag. "What about it, Lesslie?"

"A cardiac ultrasound would help us with that," I ventured. "Some of the congenital problems don't manifest themselves until a little time has passed."

As soon as I made that statement I regretted it. He was going to ask me to name a few and when they usually declare themselves.

"That's a thought," he said instead. "We have to quickly go through a list of potential diagnoses here and come up with the ones that seem most likely. What can cause weakness and poor muscle tone in a child this age? Infection, cardiac, metabolic. Elevated levels of magnesium. Had the mother received this during labor and delivery for a hypertensive problem? That could cause these findings. But that would have happened shortly after birth. As would the findings of neonatal myasthenia gravis. An interesting possibility, but the mother almost always has the disease, and the referring physician should have known about that. But this child is three months old and had been in previous good health. Where does that leave us?"

Lipsky went through an impressive list of possible causes for these findings—most of them obscure and unlikely. An infection in the child's brain or a stroke were possibilities, and we would be getting a scan of his head as soon as he was stable enough to go to radiology. But those were improbable causes for his condition, as were some of the paralysis syndromes. A drug ingestion was a possibility, and we would need to question his mother about this. But at three months of age, he wasn't crawling around and getting into medicine bottles.

"What about alcohol?" Simmons ventured. "Not necessarily intentional, but accidental? We've seen it happen before with colicky babies. The parents will try almost anything to stop the crying."

"Hmm…" Lipsky mused. "A good thought, but it wouldn't explain the low temperature and constipation. But a thought, nonetheless."

Cecil's heart rate had improved with a bolus of IV fluids, and his temperature was rising with warming blankets and a heat lamp. But he remained listless and minimally responsive. We needed an answer, and fast.

"I think we can anticipate a ventilator," Lipsky said, looking at Simmons. "His respiratory muscles will fatigue, and he'll be in trouble. Are you comfortable in securing his airway?"

John didn't hesitate. "Sure. When do you want that to happen?"

Cecil was breathing and his oxygen saturation was normal, but he looked tired. He would need to be intubated sooner rather than later.

"Let's get everything ready." Lipsky turned and walked to the nurses' station.

The swarm of activity had settled into a controlled and purposeful flow. And while Cecil continued to be the main focus of our efforts and attention, the other 20 newborns in the unit needed care as well. So much for the quiet afternoon.

Maybelle slowly got up from her rocker, carefully cradling the blanketed bundle in her arms. She quietly made her way through the maze of incubators to her child's bassinet, brushing me gently as she passed.

"Honey," she whispered.

What had she said? Honey?

"Ask about honey." She nodded and walked away.

"Honey." I murmured the word.

Simmons's head snapped around. "What was that, Robert? Did you say honey?"

Lipsky looked up from the chart in his hand. He dropped it to the countertop and walked over to us.

"Honey." He uttered the word slowly, and it hung in the air. "Is that your idea, Dr. Lesslie?"

"Well...I...it was..." I glanced over at Maybelle. Her back was to me, and she didn't turn around.

"That's a very real possibility." Lipsky folded his arms across his chest and nodded. "If Cecil's mother has been giving him local honey—unpasteurized—this could very well be a case of infantile botulism. Good thought there, Lesslie."

What? Botulism? I had read about it, and our college biology professor had thought it important enough to include it on a couple of exams...but botulism? In an infant?

Simmons looked at me with raised eyebrows, and my face flamed.

"As soon as Cecil's mother gets here, we'll need to find out what she's been feeding him," he said. "And if it's honey..."

Fifteen minutes later, she was standing beside his incubator—pale and fidgeting.

"Is he going to be all right? He's not bad sick, is he? I mean..."

John Simmons asked her a multitude of questions—family history, her experience during pregnancy, labor, and delivery...and then about honey.

"Yes, I give him a little honey each day," she answered. "I've given it to all my other kids when they were about his age. Somethin' my grandma told me would help them get stronger and all. But only the stuff that's harvested around where we live. The local honey is supposed to help with allergies, I think."

Lipsky was standing at the nurses' station, and when he heard this, he turned to the unit secretary. "Call the pharmacy and get us BIG, IV, and stat. I don't care what they have to do to get it—I want it here in ten minutes."

She shook her head. "Big?" It was something we didn't order very often—maybe never.

"Botulism immune globulin. They'll know, and tell them to hurry."

Infantile botulism is caused by the bacterium *Clostridium botulinum*, a commonly occurring organism found in the soil. It forms spores, which can end up in ingested dirt or even honey and some corn syrups. As adults, we probably come across this frequently, but we're able to handle small amounts of it. In infants a few weeks to six months old, the spores can "hatch" in the GI tract, and the bacteria then produces the poison that causes botulism. Symptoms include constipation, weakness and lethargy, drooping eyelids, poor feeding, and finally paralysis and respiratory failure. Everything we were seeing with Cecil.

He received the lifesaving antidote in time, and within a matter of hours he had improved to the point where we could all take a deep breath. But it had been close. Too close.

Two days later, we were finishing our afternoon rounds, and I was making some notations in the chart of one of our new admissions. The faint notes of a familiar refrain caught my ear, and I turned to the corner of the room. Maybelle rocked quietly, softly humming as she held a small child in her arms.

Cecil.

"Let not your heart be troubled,"
His tender word I hear,
And resting on His goodness, I lose my doubts and fear;
Though by the path He leadeth, but one step I may see,
His eye is on the sparrow, and I know He watches me;
His eye is on the sparrow, and I know He watches me.

CIVILLA D. MARTIN, "HIS EYE IS ON THE SPARROW"

6

A Seed Planted

Fifteen minutes. That's all you get.

After that, fresh-brewed coffee starts to lose its flavor—or at least that's what the "experts" say. Highway patrolman Jay Manning and I stared at the half-empty pot resting on the warmer in the lounge. Its color was suspect, but it was three in the morning and all we had.

"You first." I waved at the pot, handed him a Styrofoam cup, and slumped into a chair.

I was tired. The evening had been busy, and at midnight, EMS 1 had brought in a couple of teenagers from an auto accident. Nothing serious other than a few bruises and lacerations that needed repair. But both of the young men had been drinking and narrowly missed disaster when their pickup truck skidded to a stop barely inches from a huge and unforgiving pine tree. That's what had brought Jay Manning to the ER—the MVA (motor vehicular accident) and the boys' blood alcohol levels.

"Nice try with those kids," Jay said. "I think one of them might have been listening."

While suturing one teenager's forehead, I had taken the opportunity to offer him some fatherly advice about the realities of drinking and driving. His friend was reclining on a nearby stretcher, his eyes closed and his mouth open and slack. I didn't think he was hearing much of anything.

"I've given that speech too many times before, and I'll probably give it too many times in the future," I replied. "Those boys were lucky tonight, but it doesn't always turn out that way. You know that as well as I do—maybe better."

Jay sighed and nodded. "You're right, but you've got to try. You never know when something you say will take root and make a difference. Who knows? Maybe that kid will change his ways. Wouldn't that be something?"

Jay studied the coffee cup in his hands, shook his head at the stale java, and placed it on the nearby counter.

"Let me tell you about Sylvia Bannister."

It was two days before Christmas 1983, and Jay Manning was responding to a 10-50 on Highway 21, right as it passed over the Catawba River. Single vehicle auto accident was the call. Unknown injuries.

EMS 1 was on the way, but they were still at the hospital, and it would be at least ten minutes before they could get to the scene. Local police were a couple of miles away and en route. Jay was just down the road and the first to arrive.

Midnight, and the highway was nearly deserted. Jay's flashing blue lights reflected off the rear bumper of a late-model Impala, and he rolled to a stop a few yards behind the car. No sign of the driver, who appeared to have veered off the two-lane road and straight into the concrete post that marked the beginning of the river bridge. The post had won, and the front of the Impala was wrapped around the marker, which seemed mostly unscathed by the assault.

Jay grabbed his flashlight and jumped out of the cruiser. In the distance he could hear the wail of approaching sirens—the city police and EMS 1.

He raced to the driver's side of the car and directed the beam of his light through the front window. A young woman, probably in her thirties, slumped back in the seat, her hands still clutching the steering wheel. The windshield was splintered, and he saw pieces of glass stippling her bleeding forehead.

"Ma'am, are you all right?"

He thought it was a stupid question, since she had just run into a bridge. But what else are you going to say?

A rivulet of blood coursed into her right eye and down her cheek. She managed to partially open her left eye and peered up at the patrolman.

"Am I alive?"

Odd question, and Jay was about to answer when EMS 1 roared up behind him, crunching loose gravel on the side of the road and sending it flying.

"What ya got, Jay?" One of the paramedics bounded out of the ambulance, grabbed his medical box, and quickly strode to the side of the Impala.

"Just got here," Jay answered. "Single car, it looks like. And there's no one else in the vehicle. I'll get out of your way and start checking the scene."

The patrolman hadn't detected the smell of alcohol in the car, and he had been pretty close to the woman. Still, that was yet to be determined. But she could have been dodging an animal in the road or momentarily looking away.

He was standing 20 yards behind the car with his flashlight sweeping the asphalt and the graveled shoulder. He froze and leaned closer to the highway.

There were no brake marks on the road—none in the gravel. Jay retraced his steps to the rear of the Impala, turned around, and paced slowly back up the highway. Fifty yards and nothing. The driver hadn't made any attempt to avoid the bridge post, but just plowed right into it.

The two paramedics had extricated the woman from her car. They loaded her onto their stretcher and were wheeling her into the back of the ambulance. Jay walked over to them.

"She looks okay," one of the paramedics said. "Vital signs are fine and no evidence of any significant head or neck injury. Might have broken her right kneecap where it hit the dash, but if that's all she has wrong, she'll be mighty lucky."

The ambulance doors slammed shut. Jay stood there, his eyes moving from the ambulance to the crushed Impala.

"I'll see you guys in the ER," he said. "Just want to take a look around some more."

EMS 1 did a U-turn in the middle of Highway 21, fired up their lights and siren, and sped off in the direction of the hospital.

"Odd," Jay muttered.

The ER doctor walked out of the Trauma room and over to the nurses' station. Jay Manning was waiting for her.

"What do you think, Doc? Is she going to be okay?"

"Well, she's lucky other than having a fractured right patella." (There was that word again—"lucky.") "But that's all I can find. All of her other X-rays are good, and she's awake and alert. I'll need to put a few sutures in her forehead, but you can go talk with her before I get started. She's not saying much, though, and doesn't remember anything about the accident. Doesn't even remember seeing the bridge."

She had just started making some notes on the woman's chart when her hand froze in midair. "Oh, and her blood alcohol is zero. Nada. So that's not an explanation for the accident. We may never know what caused her to hit that post."

Jay turned and headed toward the open door of the Trauma room.

"Sylvia Bannister," the ER doc called over her shoulder. "Her name is Sylvia Bannister."

The doctor had been right. Sylvia didn't have much to say. She answered questions about her date of birth and where she lived, but that was about it. She didn't remember anything about the accident, or at least didn't want to talk about it.

One of the ortho-techs was placing a splint around her injured right knee as Jay finished up his report.

He signed the slip of paper, carefully tore it from his pad, and placed it on the counter beside Sylvia's stretcher.

"This is your copy, so be sure you have it when you leave the hospital. There won't be any charges, and I hope that everything heals fine and that you'll be okay."

Sylvia stared at the wall in front of her and didn't say anything.

"And if you need any information, my name and number are on that report. Just give me a call."

Still nothing.

Jay turned and walked out of the room.

Two months later, another call was dispatched for an emergency on Highway 21. It was at the same bridge over the Catawba River, and it was again a little after midnight. Jay Manning was on duty and patrolling a little over a mile away. He hadn't heard the nature of the emergency, but he was close by, so he headed in that direction.

The night was bitterly cold with a chance of early morning frozen precipitation. That was going to be a disaster for South Carolina drivers, and he was glad his shift would be ending at six o'clock.

He pulled up to the entrance of the bridge, remembering the encounter with Sylvia Bannister. Jay had followed up on her after the accident, and from what he had gathered, she had recovered without any more problems. Or none that he heard about.

Once again, he was the first person arriving at the scene. The patrolman stopped a few feet from the concrete pole that had brought Sylvia's Impala to a sudden stop. He got out of his car, and the beam of his flashlight reflected off chunks of cement still lying on the ground. He looked up and scanned the 300 yards of the two-lane bridge. Nothing— no vehicle, no lights. Nothing.

Jay reached into the car for his radio to call Dispatch to make sure he was in the right place when two headlights sped toward him. The frigid February night was pierced by the blaring horn of an approaching car.

He pressed himself into the side of the patrol car as the driver slammed on his brakes and shimmied to a stop beside him.

"Officer, you've got to get back there and do something!"

The driver looked to be in his early twenties, and his wide eyes flitted from Jay to something on the road behind him. He jerked his thumb in the same direction and repeated, "You got to do something!"

Jay looked back down the bridge, peering through the darkness to see something—anything.

"What are you—" The car sped away before he could finish his question.

Jay grabbed his radio, called for backup—for what, he didn't know—and then patted his hip, making sure his service weapon was where it should be.

There were no other vehicles on the bridge, and the night was eerily quiet. *Where is EMS? Or the police?* In spite of the ten-degree temperature, Jay Manning broke into a sweat.

He hurried down the right-hand side of the bridge, lamenting the age of the structure and its lack of any substantial shoulder. He swung the flashlight from side to side, searching for anything unusual, anything suspicious—or dangerous.

Jay was almost in the middle of the bridge when he saw it. Just up ahead, a pale figure reflected the bright beam of his light. He paused and squinted his eyes, trying to comprehend what he was seeing.

The rails on the sides of the bridge were only about two feet tall, regularly interspersed with a slightly taller rectangular concrete pillar. The figure up ahead was standing on the side of the bridge, leaning against...No! Someone was standing on one of the pillars and staring down into the blackness below.

Jay hurried his pace and kept his light focused on the figure. When he was within 30 yards, he could make out the shape of a woman, dressed only in a thin shirt and slacks. As he drew closer, the woman turned her head and faced him. He stopped dead in his tracks.

Sylvia Bannister.

Her eyes were empty and listless, and she raised a slender arm, her palm cautioning him to come no closer.

"I'll jump." The words were almost lost in the cold night, but he had heard them. And he believed her.

"Sylvia, we can talk about this."

Her head jerked a little in his direction, and she studied his face.

Recognition flickered for a moment in her eyes, and then she said again, "I'll jump."

Jay knew the bridge, and he knew the river. He had spent his early years fishing its banks and canoeing this stretch. It was a least a 100-foot drop to shallow water and exposed rocks. If Sylvia jumped, she would die.

He remembered her accident and the lack of brake marks on the highway. Now he understood why he had felt uneasy that night and why things hadn't made sense. It had been no accident. She had tried to take her own life, and here she was again. Only this time, unless he stopped her, she would succeed.

"Sylvia, listen. Let's talk for just a minute. I won't come any closer, I promise. But tell me what—"

And she was gone. Her eyes never left his. She just took a step into the abyss and disappeared.

No scream, no last-minute cries for help. Just the darkness below, and a strange and final thump as she landed.

Two police cars pulled up, followed by an ambulance.

"What's going on here, Jay?" One of the officers approached him. "I don't see a wreck or anything. Why did you need backup?"

Jay's flashlight was pointing to the ground. Slowly, he raised it to the now-empty pillar on the side of the bridge.

"We'll need the rescue squad," he said quietly. "And the coroner."

When Jay told the gathering group what had happened, one of the paramedics ran back to his ambulance and grabbed his own flashlight—big and powerful. He walked over to the rail and began searching the rocks below.

"Jay, don't beat yourself up over this," one of the officers said. "It sounds like this woman was determined to kill herself, and nothing you or anyone else could have done was going to change that. Sometimes—"

"Hey, come take a look at this!"

The paramedic with the flashlight was leaning dangerously over one of the rails and shining his light directly below them.

"See, right over there!"

The icy water of the Catawba River gurgled and splashed around a thousand lethal rocks and ledges, and it took a moment for Jay to focus on the object of the paramedic's excited attention. Right below them was a tangle of dead tree limbs and branches, caught in one of the many eddies of the river. And on top of that pile of debris was the body of Sylvia Bannister. And she was moving.

Rock Hill Rescue arrived moments later and quickly got her off the pile, out of the river, and into the waiting ambulance. She was shivering but awake and looking around. One of her wrists was broken, as were several ribs. But she was moving everything, and there was no evidence of a head or neck injury. Lucky—again.

Jay was standing at the back of the ambulance, and when the paramedic jumped out, he leaned in, close enough for Sylvia to hear his quiet words.

"Sylvia, I don't know what's going on in your life that would make you want to end it. It's none of my business, but as sure as we're on this bridge in the middle of February, the Lord doesn't want this to happen. This is twice now that He's kept you alive. You need to think about that and be thankful. And you need to figure out what He has in mind for you, 'cause it's something. This is more than luck. Much more."

"Jay, what a story!" I told him. "That's incredible! I've canoed down that part of the river too, and when the water's low, you can barely get through. And those rocks *are* deadly."

"Wait just a minute." He raised a hand and leaned forward in his chair. "That's not all."

"What? There's more?"

"The most important part. Sylvia Bannister was admitted to the hospital that night and got the psychiatric care she needed. But she needed more than that, and we both knew it. I lost track of her for a while, but didn't get any more calls in the middle of the night to the Catawba River Bridge. Then one evening I took my wife and kids to the Sagebrush for dinner. We were sitting at our table, eating peanuts, when up walks Sylvia. She's the manager of the place. She saw me across the restaurant and came over to say hello and to thank me. She said what I told her that night in the back of the ambulance had started her thinking, and it was the beginning of things turning around for her." Jay paused and cleared his throat. "But it wasn't me she needed to be thanking, and we both knew it."

We were silent for a few minutes, Jay reliving this experience, and me thinking about the teenage boys from the auto accident.

"I guess I'll keep giving these young people what little advice I have. Maybe, just maybe, a word or two will take hold."

Jay looked at me and nodded. "You just never know."

The soothing tongue is a tree of life.

Proverbs 15:4

7

A Charmed Life

S ome people work hard all their lives and never catch a break. Others wander through this world bathed in the sunlight of good fortune. And then there's Charlie Whitesell.

ER, Friday afternoon

The police officer walked through the triage entrance and straight to the nurses' station. Connie, one of the nurses on duty, stood beside me. She hadn't seen or heard the young man approach.

He put his arm around her waist, pulled her close, and said, "Hello, sweetheart."

Nobody looked up or reacted in any way. After all, Connie was Charlie Whitesell's wife—for all of six months.

"Luckiest guy I know," another police officer had remarked upon the announcement of their engagement. "I've been tryin' for a year to get her to go out with me, but nothin' doin'. Same for half the police force. Like I said, the luckiest guy I know."

There might have been some luck involved, but with Charlie, there was also planning, opportunity, and timing. The timing was the most important part, and Charlie had a knack.

Halloween night, one year earlier

It was a little after 11 p.m., and the second-shift crew was heading home. They had given their report to those working graveyard, and they were tired and beaten down from a busy evening.

Lori Davidson pulled on her coat and stopped beside me behind the nurses' station.

"What a crazy night," she sighed. "But then again, it's Halloween. What should we expect, right?"

"I wasn't expecting that group of college students who came in stoned," I responded. "What was it—ten or twelve of them? And they claimed they didn't know who baked the brownies that just happened to be laced with marijuana. Must have been from the Junior Welfare League Cookbook."

Lori chuckled. "At least nobody got hurt. Charlie Whitesell saw to that. I don't know how he knew something was going on at that fraternity house, but he did. Just like he always does. Brought them in before anything got out of hand or someone took off driving and got hurt—or worse."

The ambulance doors opened, and we both looked up.

"Well, speak of the devil," I said.

Charlie walked over to us, the familiar grin spreading across his face.

"Just got all those kids taken care of," he said. "I think they've learned a lesson tonight."

"You didn't believe that stuff about not knowing how the marijuana got in those brownies?" Lori squinted at him and cocked her head to one side.

"Of course not," he answered, shaking his head. "But under the circumstances and with most of the evidence gone—or eaten—we cut them some slack. Still, they were pretty scared, and I don't think they'll forget what happened."

He looked around the department. "Anyway, I just came back to—"

Singing. Loud singing.

We all turned and stared down the hallway. The unmistakable words of Aretha Franklin's "Respect" echoed off the walls, seconds before their source rounded the corner by the Ortho room.

It was Connie Taylor, one of our night nurses. She moved languidly up the hall, her arms making wide, sweeping arcs above her head.

"I ain't gonna do you wrong while you're gone."

The words were unmistakable but a little slurred.

Connie strutted toward us, and when only a few feet away, pointed her finger in the police officer's face and rhythmically chanted, "Re, re, re, re, re, re, re, respect."

She stood theren swaying and singing, and we stared—Lori's eyes as wide as the headlights of Charlie's patrol car.

Connie paused at the end of a verse, and her arms dropped to her sides. Her eyes were half-closed and she smiled, still swaying to the music of an unseen band.

"Hmm." Charlie reached out and gently brushed some dark-brown crumbs from her left cheek.

"As I was about to say," he casually commented, "I just came back to get the rest of the evidence. I think I left a couple of brownies wrapped up in tinfoil back in the lounge. Looks like this young woman might have found them."

Connie smiled and swayed. Charlie took her by her shoulders and guided her back down the hallway to the lounge.

Lori took off her coat, dropped it on the counter, and followed them.

"I'll take care of her," Lori said as she passed me.

And that's how Charlie met Connie. He didn't exactly save her life, but he probably did save her job—and her dignity. It wasn't too many months later that he gave her his last name.

But there's more to Charlie's good luck and good fortune than how he managed to confuse and capture Connie Taylor. A lot more. Let's start with Benny Bostic.

Police Chief Dan Carothers pulled Charlie Whitesell aside after the morning report.

"Charlie, I'm going to ask you to do something, and while you might disagree, it's important. Trust me."

This wasn't a good way to start a conversation, and Charlie folded his arms across his chest.

A highly placed individual in the city government had a nephew—an aspiring young police officer. He had just finished training, and though he hadn't exactly impressed his instructors, he still had some promise. Or at least his uncle thought so.

"All he needs is a little experience, Dan," the uncle had cajoled Chief Carothers. "It will certainly be appreciated."

"Wait a minute." Charlie stared at his chief, backing away. "You're not talking about Benny Bostic, are you? I've got some friends at the academy, and they were telling me some stuff about—"

"Hold on." Carothers grabbed Charlie's shoulder, trying to calm him. "Yes, it's Benny Bostic, but it's only for two weeks—maybe three. That's all I promised his uncle. Then we'll move him somewhere else, somewhere he can't…"

"Where he can't *what?*" Charlie was worried now. The things he had heard about Benny's performance at the academy were mostly benign—occasionally oversleeping and missing mandatory classes, often misplacing paperwork, generally being clumsy, and overall lacking attention to detail. Not the kind of things you wanted in a partner. But what was the chief alluding to?

"Two weeks, Charlie. That's all I'm asking."

It turned out to be even less than that, but those few days almost proved to be too much for Charlie.

The third day of their patrolling turned out to be pivotal. Charlie was driving, as he always was.

"Keep a sharp lookout," he told Benny. For what, he really didn't know. But he *did* know he wasn't about to put his life in Bostic's hands behind the wheel of the patrol car.

"All available units respond to an armed robbery at 218 West Hampton."

Benny spun in his seat and stared openmouthed at Charlie.

"Calm down. That's a mile from here, and we probably won't be the first unit to get there. But let's go."

Lights and siren and they were on their way.

Their patrol car *was* the first to arrive, just in time to see an armed and masked figure backing out of the doorway of a small convenience store.

Charlie switched off the car, grabbed his service weapon, and opened the door. He glanced over at Benny. "Stay behind me and don't do anything crazy."

Charlie jumped out of the car and approached the perpetrator, who was now standing in the sidewalk, facing the officers.

"Don't come any closer." The muffled voice came from beneath the mask. "I'm not afraid to use this." He waved his gun in the air and then pointed it straight at Charlie.

Whitesell heard a metallic click behind him, and his body stiffened. Benny had cocked his gun. Charlie waved his empty hand behind him, trying to signal the young officer to calm down.

Charlie spoke loudly and firmly to the armed robber. "Listen to me. This doesn't have to end with you dying. Drop that gun and put your hands behind your head."

It was a standoff, and the only sounds Charlie heard were the gasping breaths of Benny Bostic.

More sirens, and three patrol cars rocketed into the street, surrounding the robber and cutting off any chance of escape. Police officers flooded the pavement and sidewalk—every weapon trained on the masked man.

Finally, "Okay, okay." He dropped his gun and raised both hands. "Okay."

Seconds later he was on the ground—cuffed, secure, and alive.

It was over. Almost.

Charlie turned around and faced the barrel of Benny Bostic's weapon. They were ten feet apart, and the new recruit stood frozen and pale.

"What's the matter, Benny? Holster your weapon."

"I can't," Benny mumbled. "It's cocked, and I don't know how to uncock it."

What?

Charlie stared at his inept pupil and realized he was dead serious. He took a deep breath and raised his right hand, palm facing the business end of the firearm.

"All right, Benny, listen. Put your thumb on the hammer, pull the trigger gently, and ease the hammer back down. That's all you need to do. Okay?"

Benny nodded. "Put my thumb on the hammer…pull the trigger…"

Bam!

Charlie ducked, but not before he heard and felt the bullet whizz past his left ear.

An hour later, he was walking into Captain Carothers's office.

"Charlie, I heard, and I'm—"

Charlie raised his hand to silence the chief. Without a word, he dropped Benny's service weapon onto Carothers's desk, turned, and walked out.

"Momma said there'd be days like this…" and there were others. Though he lived a charmed life, strange and unforeseen occurrences followed Charlie like pigeons on bread crumbs.

Two a.m. and Charlie was alone, driving his patrol car west on Cherry Road. The light at the intersection with Heckle Boulevard turned red and he braked, thankful for a brief rest.

It had been a terrible evening. A well-known and much respected elderly couple had been murdered in their sleep. There was no obvious motive, nothing missing in the house—just a brutal and senseless

killing. The two offenders hadn't been very careful in covering
trail and had been apprehended within hours. Marty Fuller and Jere.
Tyson—both well known to the Rock Hill police force. Tyson's part
in this hadn't come as a surprise to anyone. He was flat-out mean and
didn't care about anything. Fuller, on the other hand, had some run-
ins with the law but nothing serious. His biggest mistake was picking
the wrong friends.

"If you lie down with dogs, you'll rise up with fleas," Chief Carothers liked to say.

The light turned green, and Charlie eased forward, preparing to
make a left turn onto Heckle. He glanced at the dinged and dented
Ford pickup that was stopped at the light in the lane beside him, headed
north.

The driver of the truck ducked but not before their eyes locked on
each other.

It couldn't be!

Charlie slammed on the brakes as the pickup burned rubber and
ran the red light.

The radio squawked as Charlie spun the wheel as hard as he could.
"All units, be on the lookout for an escapee. Jeremy Tyson."

It was him! How had he…

Charlie completed his U-turn, flipped on his lights and siren, and
took off after the disappearing taillights of the Ford.

He was breathing hard, and his face was flushed.

"Dispatch, this is Unit 3," he spoke into the radio. "I'm in pursuit of
a 1995 Ford Ranger, headed north on Heckle. It's Jeremy Tyson, and
I'm requesting backup."

He dropped the radio on the passenger seat and shook his head.
Tyson had been jailed a bunch of times and had broken out on at least
three different occasions—maybe four. How could it happen again?

A couple of units responded from the other side of town—15 or
more minutes away. A lone sheriff's deputy radioed in, but he was down
in Catawba, and it would be a while before he could help.

d his grip on the wheel and slammed his foot to the

to get away.

through the night, first down Heckle and then
...g snarply onto a smaller road that headed out into the country.
Charlie was still a good distance behind him, but he was closing.

The chase continued for five miles, then ten. Tyson came to an intersection and made a hard left, cutting a corner through a gas station. He clipped a gas pump that rattled off into the parking lot before coming to rest against a picnic table on the side of the small building. Tyson managed to bring the Ranger back onto the highway.

Charlie watched all of this happen while making a more controlled turn at the light. He waited for the fiery explosion. Nothing. The store and intersection disappeared into blackness behind him.

Jeremy Tyson never slowed down—not until he overshot a sharp left turn and met an unforgiving barbed-wire fence. The truck came to an awkward rest on its passenger side, and Tyson scrambled out his window, over the front of the truck, and into a 50-acre field of three-foot-high soybeans.

Charlie pulled up beside the wrecked Ranger, picked up his radio, thought better of it, and tossed it aside. He grabbed a flashlight, made sure his service weapon was in its holster, and jumped out of the car.

The ocean of soybeans in front of him was a tight, dark mass. Charlie stood at the edge of the field and listened. Off somewhere to his right, he heard thrashing and labored grunting. The beam of his light swept across the field and came to rest on the back of Jeremy Tyson, 50 yards away. The fugitive glanced over his shoulder, changed direction, and kept running.

Charlie unholstered his weapon and bolted into the soybeans.

Running through this stuff was difficult—like trying to jog in the surf at the beach. And Tyson was getting away. Charlie redoubled his efforts, mangling the plants as he ran over and through them. All the while, he somehow kept his light focused on Tyson. To lose sight of him now would be dangerous—even deadly.

He was getting closer—maybe because he was running as hard as he could or because Tyson was slowing down. But he was getting closer. The escaped killer stopped and spun around. He bent over, grabbed his knees, and gasped for breath.

"Don't shoot!" he wheezed. "I ain't armed."

Charlie slowed a little but kept running toward the man. His firearm and flashlight were both aimed at the slumping figure.

Tyson slowly stood and raised empty hands. He wasn't a big man, and Charlie had taken down men twice his size. The officer stopped 15 feet away and reached for his handcuffs.

"Put your hands behind your head and get down on your knees."

A siren screamed in the dark distance. Tyson glanced in its direction and then back at the police officer. He didn't move.

"I said put your hands behind your head and—"

Tyson was gone. He had taken two giant strides and ducked beneath the surface of the soybeans. Gone.

Charlie scanned the tops of the beans with his flashlight, searching for any movement. Nothing…and no noise. Tyson wasn't moving. He was waiting.

The siren was getting closer—two of them now. But Charlie had to do something. He took a couple of steps straight ahead, stopped, and listened again.

Nothing.

Then the crush of trampled bushes, and Tyson was on him. Charlie's flashlight flew into the air and landed ten feet away, hidden by the dense plants. And his firearm…where was it?

Tyson had his arm locked around Charlie's neck. The two men rolled over each other, flattening the soybeans, their stems poking eyes and ears.

A short, powerful uppercut, and Charlie was free. Another blow, and Tyson was on his back, staring into the night sky.

Charlie straddled the man's chest and cuffed him.

"You have the right to remain…oh, what the heck."

Fifteen minutes later, the lights of five patrol cars flooded the field and the side of the road. Tyson was being shown the back of one of the cars, and Charlie leaned against the hood of another, nursing a multitude of scrapes and bruises.

"You are one lucky guy," one of his friends remarked.

Charlie looked over at him and gently rubbed a bruised lip.

"Yeah," the officer continued. "I guess he didn't want to fire his gun, maybe thinking it would bring us all down on him."

"What gun?" Charlie stood still, searching the officer's face.

"This one." He held up an evidence bag containing a small .32 caliber revolver. Loaded. "And he had these." Another bag with two knives— one a switchblade and the other a mean-looking hawkbill.

"Yeah, you're one lucky guy."

Charlie knew he was. But he also knew not to push it, not to press his luck. At least not until he heard Lucius Tolbert was out of prison.

Tolbert had been locked up for seven years, convicted of a multitude of sins and transgressions. Armed robbery, attempted homicide, breaking and entering…Name it, and it was probably on his rap sheet. No one understood how he got out of prison, considering his convictions and the nature of his crimes. But the word was out that he was once more on the street and had resumed his duties as "president" of one of the area's biker gangs. In prison, his name Lucius became Lucifer—fitting, but he preferred the nickname given him years earlier by his gang: the Hammer.

While incarcerated, he had made contact with some innovative and clever criminals. He learned some things and was eager to put them into practice. A few months after his release, a new and dangerous crime wave confronted the police department of Rock Hill, and Charlie Whitesell was studying an alarming and recurring pattern.

"Chief, I think these liquor store robberies are the work of one man— or maybe a team. And I think Lucius Tolbert is involved."

"I don't know, Charlie. That would be pretty brazen, don't you think?

The guy's just out of prison, and if he gets into any kind of trouble, he'll be going back. And this time, they'll throw away the key."

"Should have done that last time," Charlie opined. "But this has his hand all over it. Thirteen robberies in four weeks. And each with the same MO. A big, masked guy walks in the store, pulls out a gun, demands money and car keys, steals the storekeeper's car, and takes off. Doesn't leave a car behind, and we don't know who's dropping him off, but every time it's the same thing. And he knows these storekeepers always have some kind of a weapon behind the counter. He steals those too and uses them at the next holdup, and then the guns disappear. Smart. We can find the cars, but it's no use to trace them. We know who they belong to, and there are never any prints. I'm telling you, this has to be the Hammer."

Carothers sighed and rubbed his chin.

"I don't know," the chief mused, studying the top of his desk. "But your hunches are usually right. I'll give you a week to try to find this guy and follow him. If something turns up, you call it in, right? He's trouble, and I want you to be careful. Take Walt Letson with you. He's done this kind of thing before, and he's got a level head."

Charlie turned to the door and put a hand on the knob. "Thanks, Chief."

"Be careful, you hear?"

A week passed, and another liquor store robbery had gone down.

Charlie had been patrolling with Walt Letson. The chief had been right—Walt knew what he was doing, and he and Charlie made a good team.

They were the first to respond to the robbery. Same MO—a large, masked man had burst in with a sawed-off shotgun and demanded the storekeeper's money and car keys.

"What about a weapon?" Charlie asked the man behind the counter. "Do you keep a firearm of some sort in the store?"

The 60-year-old-man grunted and shook his head. "That really ticks me off. He came behind the counter and grabbed my Clint Eastwood special."

"Clint Eastwood—" Walt began, but Charlie interrupted.

"You have a Smith and Wesson Model 29?"

"Had," the storekeeper sighed. "Had a Model 29. That guy stole it. Just like Dirty Harry's but bigger—the barrel's eight and three-quarter inches."

"That's a cannon!" Charlie looked the man up and down. Five feet five at the most and maybe 125 pounds. The recoil would have knocked him down.

"You said he took your car keys," Walt pursued. "What kind of car do you drive?"

"A 2005 Nissan. Green with a dented rear fender. My wife…oh, never mind."

"Thanks," Charlie told him. "We're gonna get right on it."

The two officers got back in their patrol car, and Charlie fired up the engine.

"I got an idea," he told Walt. "One of the guys that works narcotics heard that Lucius Tolbert has been seeing a young lady—Candy DeVito. She lives over in East Lake Estates with her parents. I'm not sure about the address, but I think we need to pay her a visit."

It was six o'clock, and dusk was settling over Rock Hill as they drove into the quiet, manicured neighborhood.

"Not exactly the kind of place you'd expect to find the Hammer," Walt said. His eyes scanned the passing driveways and garages.

"This guy's smart," Charlie responded. "This would be a good place for him to hang out."

Walt raised his hand and pointed up the street. Parked at the curb on the right-hand side of the road was a green Nissan.

Charlie slowed and stopped right behind the car.

"Dented rear fender," Walt said quietly.

"And it looks like a 2005," Charlie added. "Call for backup, and let's check it out."

The two men got out of the patrol car, separated, and approached the front of the house.

The front door burst open, and out stepped the Hammer.

"Well, well," he laughed. "If it isn't little Charlie Whitesell come to visit. And who's your little friend here?"

They didn't have an arrest warrant—only a hunch—and Charlie knew they needed to go slow.

"Lucius, we'd like to talk with you for a minute. Mind if we come in?" Tolbert stiffened and glanced behind him. Something was wrong. He pulled the door closed and put his right hand behind his back.

"Lucius, put your hands where we can see them," Charlie ordered.

A look not unlike that of Lucifer spread across the Hammer's face. His massive frame hunched over, and now both hands were behind his back, struggling to find something.

"What the—"

Charlie drew his weapon and aimed it at the middle of the Hammer's chest. Walt sprang from where he stood, drove his shoulder into the man's chest—knocking the air out of him—and rode him to the ground. Something clattered on the sidewalk, and Charlie looked down—the Smith and Wesson. He pounced, and they had the Hammer cuffed and on his belly in less than a minute.

They stood over him, panting. Sirens approached, shattering the calm of the neighborhood.

"How did you do that?" Charlie asked his partner.

"I guess the chief neglected to tell you I was a state champion wrestler," Walt answered.

"No, he neglected to tell me you were crazy."

Help arrived, and Charlie turned to Walt. "We need to check on this Candy person and her parents."

They walked into the house and through the living room. They froze when they reached the arched opening to the dining room.

Candy DeVito and her parents, John and Bernice, were bound and gagged with duct tape to wooden, straight-backed chairs. Terrified, but alive.

Charlie's hunch had saved them.

Luck or a charmed life?
If you asked Charlie, he'd smile and say, "I just always try to be ready."

Shallow men believe in luck.
Strong men believe in cause and effect.

RALPH WALDO EMERSON

8

Another Look

Aaron Brock wasn't getting any better, and his parents were long past being a little concerned. They were scared.

This was their five-year-old's third visit to the office in as many weeks. It had started with a gradually worsening cough and a low-grade fever. When it hadn't resolved in a couple of days, Amelia Brock had called for an appointment with Keith Barnwell, their family physician.

"Probably just a simple upper respiratory infection," Barnwell had explained. "We're seeing a lot of it right now, and at the worst, it might be the start of some bronchitis. I'll give him an antibiotic and something for his cough. That should do it."

A week later Aaron and his mother were back in the office. Still with cough, fever, and now some wheezing, especially at night.

"Hmm…he's never had any signs of asthma," Barnwell mused, thumbing through the young boy's chart. "And there's no family history, correct?"

"No. Dave and I were talking about that last night after Aaron started the wheezing. Nobody on his side of the family or on mine. But why would he be wheezing? Do you think he could be developing asthma?"

"A little unusual for it to manifest itself in this setting, out of the clear blue. But I suppose it's possible. Probably still the respiratory infection we treated last week. Maybe some inflammation causing narrowed airways and the wheezing we're hearing now."

He sat in front of the boy and studied him intently, noting his pale color and retracting chest wall. It had already been a week, and he should be better by now.

"Let's do this," Barnwell stood and faced Amelia Brock. "I'm going to change his antibiotic and send him to the radiology department at the hospital for a chest X-ray—just to be sure it's not pneumonia. And I'll give him something for the wheezing. Make sure he gets plenty of rest and fluids, and give him some Tylenol for his fever. We'll get him better, don't you worry."

"I hope so, Dr. Barnwell. But I *am* worried."

Barnwell found Aaron's X-ray report on his desk the next afternoon. *Normal heart size and contour. Possible early left-sided infiltrate.*

"Hmm…an early infiltrate," Barnwell mused. "Looks like Aaron's got a little pneumonia getting started."

He checked the boy's record and satisfied himself that he had put him on the right antibiotic.

"That should take care of it."

His nurse passed by, and he motioned her into his office. "Would you call Aaron Brock's mother and let her know the X-ray shows some mild pneumonia, but he's on the right medicine. I'd like to see him in a week just to be sure it's clearing up."

Barnwell handed the chart to the nurse and walked down the hall to his next patient.

Now, a week later, Aaron was back in the office with both of his parents.

"Doc, we thought he might be getting a little better a few days ago," Dave Brock began. "But this morning, when he got up and came into the kitchen to get some breakfast, he almost collapsed. He grabbed a chair and slid down to the floor. Something's going on here, and we need to find out what it is."

Keith Barnwell was startled by the boy's appearance. He had lost five pounds over the past three weeks, and his color was worse. Aaron's face was ashen, and there were dark circles beneath his listless, glassy eyes. His temperature was 102, and his respirations were shallow and labored. This was not a simple upper respiratory infection or even a mild pneumonia.

Barnwell rubbed his chin and dropped heavily into the chair beside Aaron's exam table.

"Dr. Barnwell, we have to do something." Amelia's voice was pleading, desperate.

"Yes, we do. And we will." This was beyond the family practitioner, and he knew it. He needed help. "I'm going to call the ER, and I want you to take him over there right now. Let's have them take a look at Aaron and see what they think. But be prepared for him to be admitted. I don't think they'll want to send him home."

Dave and Amelia looked at each other and then at their son.

"Whatever it takes," Amelia whispered. She moved to the exam table and put her arm around Aaron. "We just want him to get better."

Two hours later, Aaron lay on the stretcher in room 5, his eyes closed and an oxygen mask covering his nose and mouth. He was dozing in spite of the chaotic noises of the ER around him. He hadn't whimpered or made a sound when his blood was drawn—three different times—or when an IV was started in his left arm.

Kenny Lassiter, the young ER doctor on duty, had ordered another chest X-ray and was waiting at the nurses' station for it to be brought back to the department.

"What do you think's going on with the boy in 5?" Sandra Collins was the nurse taking care of Aaron, and there was an edge of worry in her voice. "His blood pressure is a little low, especially for a child his age. And we can't get his oxygen saturation above 88 percent, even with a mask."

"I don't know." Lassiter shook his head and sorted through the lab slips attached to Aaron's chart. "His white count is high—18,000—but everything else looks okay. His blood sugar is fine and so are his electrolytes. His blood urea nitrogen is a little high, which would go along with some dehydration, but we're treating that. We'll see what the X-ray shows and compare it with the one Dr. Barnwell did a week ago. That should help."

It didn't. Or at least not much. There was now a clearly visible pneumonia in Aaron's left lower lobe, and it looked like it extended into the middle lobe as well—much worse than the X-ray of a week ago. And while that gave Lassiter a working diagnosis, it didn't explain why an apparently healthy young boy was not responding to what would appear to be appropriate treatment and the correct antibiotic.

"There's something going on here," the ER doc muttered. "I just don't know what."

Amy Connors, the unit secretary, sat behind the counter at the nurses' station. "What do you think it could be?"

He looked down at her and realized he had been verbalizing his thoughts.

"This just doesn't make sense yet, and I can't quite get my head around it. I'll need to ask the family again about their medical history…whether anyone has ever had a diagnosis of cystic fibrosis or some of the genetic lung problems like alpha-1 antitrypsin deficiency."

"Alpha what?" Amy cocked her head.

"It's an inherited problem that causes a lack of protective proteins in the lungs. Frequent infections and stuff like that. It usually doesn't appear in kids his age, but I guess it's possible. I just need to go talk to them some more, let them know about the X-ray, and see if they are aware of anything that might help us out here."

He disappeared behind the curtain of room 5 and spent the next 20 minutes talking with Aaron's parents and digging for any historical piece of information that might offer some guidance.

Nothing. No family history of any lung problems or asthma. Nothing.

Lassiter walked back to the nurses' station and dropped Aaron's chart to the countertop. Behind him, the ambulance doors opened, and the paramedics of EMS 2 pushed their stretcher into the department.

"The fractured hip we called in," one of them spoke to the triage nurse. "Ortho, right?" He motioned with his head to the room in the back of the department.

"Right. If you'll take her back, I'll be there in a few minutes." The nurse handed the chart of room 5 to Amy along with an order for more blood work.

Lassiter glanced at the elderly woman as she rolled past and at her husband who walked behind the stretcher, carrying a small green suitcase. He seemed familiar, and when their eyes met, the old man smiled.

Lassiter struggled for a name or a place, but nothing came to mind.

He looked at the clock on the wall behind the nurses' station. Six thirty-five p.m. His shift would be over in another 30 minutes, and he wanted to tie up any loose ends before his relief came in. That included Aaron Brock. He was going to need to be admitted to the hospital, but Lassiter wanted a better diagnosis than pneumonia. Something more definitive if possible.

"Amy, can you get the radiologist on the phone for me? I'm going to take these films back to the department and see if they can take a look and come up with something."

"Really?" She closed her eyes and shook her head. "Do you know what time it is?"

He looked at the clock again. "Sure I know what time it is. It's only…" He let out a loud, frustrated sigh. "Oh man. It's past five and the radiologists have probably gone home. I wonder if there's a chance one of them might still be in the hospital. Why not call around and just check?"

"No use," she said flatly. "Dr. Brewster was on duty today, and I saw him head out about an hour ago when I was takin' some stuff to the lab. The lights in their office have been turned off. I can try to get the backup guys on the phone if you want."

Lassiter sighed again. "I'm not so sure about this telemetry stuff and how good they are, but okay, let's give it a try. They should at least be able to pull up both sets of films for comparison."

Amy traced the phone number written on a note stuck on a shelf in front of her and started to dial. "I wonder where these guys are sitting. From their accents, it doesn't sound like South Carolina."

"Or maybe even this hemisphere," Lassiter added. "As long as they know what they're doing, I suppose it's okay. But sometimes you just want to talk to a live person, face-to-face, and not a phone."

"Hello, this is the ER at Rock Hill General Hospital." Amy spoke into the receiver. Her eyebrows knotted, and she shook her head. "Right. Just a minute."

She handed the phone to Lassiter. "Couldn't understand much, but his first name is Doctor and his last name…I have no idea."

Lassiter took the receiver and talked with the radiologist for several minutes. There was a brief delay while the unseen and unknown physician pulled the X-rays of Aaron Brock from somewhere in the cloud. Lassiter grunted and nodded a few times, and then he handed the phone to Amy.

"What did he say?" She dropped the receiver back into its holder.

"He said it looks like a pediatric pneumonia."

"A what? Didn't you already know that?"

"Exactly."

"Well that did you a lot of good." She gathered some loose papers scattered across her work area. Her relief would also be arriving soon, and Amy wanted to leave things in as orderly a condition as possible. The usual evening shift would quickly undo those efforts.

Lassiter scratched his head and studied the top sheet of Aaron's chart.

"Amy, if you'd get the pediatrician on call for me, I'll go ahead and arrange for his admission."

Sandra Collins walked up to the nurses' station and slid some notes across the counter to Amy.

"The 87-year-old lady back in Ortho, Rachel Pressley. Looks like she's broken her right hip. I'm sure we'll need some pre-op labs and an EKG, Dr. Lassiter. Want us to go ahead and get things started?"

"What, Sandra? Oh yeah, sure." He had been thinking about Aaron Brock and needed to refocus. "I'll go back and take a look, but go ahead and get lab and X-ray down here. Thanks."

"You know who her husband is, don't you?" Sandra glanced down the hallway to the Ortho room. "That's Dr. Pressley—Ed Pressley. He's a retired radiologist. I think one of the first to come to Rock Hill."

That's why he had looked familiar to Kenny Lassiter. He had met Dr. Pressley at a hospital function a few years ago, when the retired radiologist had been receiving some kind of award. Since starting work in the ER, Lassiter had heard a lot of people talk about Dr. Pressley—that he was a good radiologist and an even better man. While the circumstances were not what any of them would have wished, the young ER doctor looked forward to talking with Dr. Pressley and his wife.

He turned and took a step in the direction of Ortho but then froze, stopped by a small voice that whispered faintly but clearly to him. Lassiter spun around and walked over to the X-ray view box. He grabbed both sets of Aaron Brock's chest X-rays and headed to the back of the department.

Rachel Pressley's right leg was shortened and turned outward. Sandra had been right—her hip was fractured, and she would soon be in the OR. In spite of her obvious pain, Rachel managed to smile and ask Lassiter about his wife and children.

"So that's the plan," he told the elderly couple after her X-rays confirmed the diagnosis. "We'll get in touch with the orthopedist on call, notify the operating room, and get you taken care of." He turned to Ed Pressley. "I know you've been around a lot of these cases, but do you have any questions? Anything we need to talk about?"

"No, I think you've covered it." Ed stood beside his wife's stretcher, holding her slender hand. "Thanks, doctor."

"Call me Kenny, sir."

Pressley chuckled. "As long as you call me Ed and not sir."

"Deal."

Lassiter had almost forgotten Aaron Brock's X-rays, which he had dropped on the chair by the door. He walked over and picked them up.

"Sir...Ed, if you don't mind, I'd like your opinion about something. Some chest X-rays of a five-year-old boy that I'm trying to sort out."

Pressley carefully placed his wife's hand on the stretcher and stepped toward Lassiter and the room's view box.

"I'd be happy to take a look, Kenny. Tell me what's going on here."

Lassiter told him everything he knew about Aaron's recent illness and the worsening pneumonia.

"He's a sick puppy, Ed, and I sense that something's going on here, but I just can't figure it out."

Ed Pressley reached into his shirt pocket and took out a battered and much-used pair of bifocals.

"Let's take a look."

He reached behind Lassiter and flipped off the room's lights. "Need all the help we can get."

Pressley peered at the first chest X-rays and then the new ones. He pursed his lips, leaned close to the films, and then looked at the initial ones again.

"Hmm...interesting." He folded his glasses and put them back in his pocket. "Where are the expiratory films?"

"The what?" Lassiter turned the lights back on. And as the room flooded with brightness, a light began to shine in Kenny's brain. And with it came a growing and welcomed relief.

"You're right, Ed. We need to get some expiratory films."

"I think they will give you the answer, Kenny. You know how that works, I'm sure. Your young patient must have aspirated some object, though for the life of me I can't see it on any of these films. When he blows out, the good lung—the right side—will get smaller. But since the left lung is blocked, it will stay the same size. And you'll have your diagnosis. The trick is going to be to figure out what's in there and then get it out."

Lassiter stared at the old man, marveling at his wisdom. He had come to the right person. But then, that small voice...

❧

It was a peanut. That was all. Yet it had almost taken the life of Aaron Brock. The inspiratory/expiratory X-rays had demonstrated exactly what Ed Pressley had predicted, and Lassiter had rushed the young boy to Charlotte to see one of the pediatric pulmonary specialists. Aaron was in the OR moments after arrival. They were able to remove the peanut, and almost immediately Aaron Brock began to improve. He was home not long after.

Lassiter had the chance to visit Ed Pressley and his wife a few days later in the hospital. He told them what had happened with Aaron and that thanks to Ed's advice, the boy would be fine.

"Ed, I don't want to think about what might have happened had I not asked you to look at those X-rays. I'll always be grateful for your help."

Pressley looked at the young ER doctor and laid a hand on his shoulder.

"The important thing, Kenny, is that for whatever reason, whatever led you to bring those X-rays to our room, you did ask. I'm glad you did. And I'm glad I could help."

A helping word to one in trouble
is often like a switch on a railroad track—
an inch between wreck and smooth-rolling prosperity.

HENRY WARD BEECHER

9

Pull Over!

Barry Weston rubbed his left shoulder and grimaced. He sighed and looked out his passenger window as the SUV sped up I-77, headed to Pineville and his family doctor. His wife, Jane, was driving, herself on the way to a doctor's appointment. It was with her oncologist—a follow-up to check on the effectiveness of recent treatments for her breast cancer.

She glanced quickly at her husband and then back at the highway. "Hurting bad?"

Barry's shoulder had been bothering him for a couple of weeks. It started after a weekend of raking oak leaves in their front yard.

"I guess I overdid it," he had told his family doctor a week later. "Thought it would be better by now, but it's getting worse. Tylenol doesn't help, nor ibuprofen. About the only thing that eases it some is to rest and hold it real still."

His doctor called it a simple muscle strain and recommended ice and something stronger for pain. He also gave Barry a muscle relaxer, which only caused him to wake up with a foggy brain.

"Yeah, pretty bad," he answered his wife. "I'm going to ask that we get some X-rays today. We've got to do something. One of the guys at work said it sounded like a rotator cuff tear. He had it happen and had the same kind of pain. Surgery fixed his, and if that's what it takes, I'm all for it."

They passed an 18-wheeler, and when clear of it, Barry saw the marker on the side of the interstate: Rest Area—2 miles.

He rubbed his shoulder again and shook his head.

As bad as his shoulder was hurting, he was more concerned about his wife. The diagnosis of breast cancer had been a gift on her fifty-first birthday—a little more than eight months ago.

"It doesn't appear to be one of the aggressive forms," her surgeon had told them. Their oncologist disagreed, and the past months had been spent with rounds of chemo and radiation. She had persevered like a champ, and Barry was proud of her. But it was taking a toll—physically and emotionally. It had to. That was the main frustration with his shoulder acting up—not the pain, but the interruption it caused. And the interference with his caring for Jane.

She looked over at him again and saw the furrowed brow and frown.

"You're not worried about this visit, are you? Dr. Whitehurst thinks I'm responding well, and I feel great. I'm not worried."

The tone of her voice belied her words.

He reached over and patted her knee.

"Oww!" His face contorted in pain, and he pulled his left arm against his chest. Another sign for the rest area—this one declaring it a half mile distant—disappeared behind them.

"Pull over." Barry pointed to the exit just ahead. "Pull over into that rest area—I've got to get out of the car."

Jane tightened her grip on the steering wheel, stole a quick glance into the rearview mirror, and flipped on the right turn signal. The SUV made a smooth exit off the interstate and headed toward several empty parking spaces in front of the low, red-brick facility.

They came to a stop, and she turned off the motor.

"Are you okay, Barry? Can I do anything?"

He grabbed the handle and pushed the door open. "I just need to get out and walk around a minute. I'll be fine. All of a sudden I just feel cooped up."

His face was pale, and sweat poured off his forehead. Barry closed the door behind him and started walking away from the SUV.

It was a gorgeous spring afternoon, and several travelers had taken advantage of the weather and the parking to enjoy some fresh air and sunshine. A dozen people sat around concrete picnic tables, and a family of four was relaxing on a gently sloping, grassy bank 20 feet away from where Jane and Barry had stopped.

He took a few steps into the parking lot, froze where he stood, and then collapsed and disappeared from Jane's sight.

She jumped out of the car and ran around the back of the SUV. Barry was lying on his side—his face a terrifying, unnatural blue. He wasn't breathing.

"Help!" Jane ran to her husband and knelt beside him on the rough asphalt surface. "Somebody help me!"

Every head within earshot turned in her direction. Most of the people didn't move, but just stared at the stricken man and his wife.

But the family sitting near them on the grassy bank all jumped up as one, and the young man sprinted to Jane's side. Without a word, he rolled her husband onto his back, laid two fingers over Barry's right carotid artery, and placed his other hand on the man's chest. No pulse, and no respiratory efforts.

The rescuer moved with swiftness and calm. He tore open Barry's shirt, positioned the man's head with his chin pointing upward, and began rhythmic, forceful chest compressions.

"We need to call 911," he instructed Jane. "Do you have a phone?"

Wide-eyed and pale, Jane wordlessly nodded. She glanced toward her car then down at her right hand. She was clutching her smartphone. Confused, she held it toward him.

A group of people was slowly coalescing around the frantic scene.

"No, you need to call them," the young man told her, growing short of breath from his efforts. His face was flushed, and sweat was already dripping down his nose. Yet his voice was calm, sure. "Call 911."

A young woman stepped beside Jane and put an arm around her shoulder. "I'm Angie Best, and that's my husband, Jason." She pointed to the man in front of them, kneeling over Barry Weston. "He's a pediatrician. Here, give me the phone and I'll call."

Jane's head swiveled from her husband to Angie and to the cell phone in her hand. She didn't speak and couldn't move.

"Here, let me have that." An elderly woman had walked up and was standing on the other side of Jane. Seventy, maybe 80 years old, she didn't wait for a response, but took the phone from Jane's hand and began dialing.

She waited for the dispatcher to answer and then spoke into the phone.

"We have a cardiac arrest—middle-aged man—no pulse or spontaneous respirations. CPR in progress. Rest area at mile marker 48."

She paused, listened, then nodded her head. "That's right, marker 48."

She looked at Jane, smiled, and handed her the phone. "Should be just a few minutes."

The woman stepped beside Jason Best, took off her sweater, and leaned next to him. "Here, raise up a second and let me put this under your knees. I know that asphalt is painful."

The pediatrician looked up at her, blew sweat off his upper lip, and whispered, "Thanks."

"I'm Edith Gettys," she told him. "Retired nurse—forty years in the ER. What can I do to help?"

She was already moving to the other side of Barry Weston, where with surprising ease she knelt and reached for Barry's head. Gently yet firmly, she took his head in her hands and repositioned his neck, allowing for the optimal movement of air into his lungs.

Jason watched her movements, nodded, and said, "That's perfect. Thanks."

"Shouldn't you be blowing in his mouth, like on TV?"

A curious onlooker had ventured near the group and rendered his opinion.

Angie Best shot a piercing glance at the man. "He knows what he's doing."

The onlooker glanced around him then shrank back into the growing crowd.

Jason Best continued his CPR. Ten minutes had passed since he'd started. Then fifteen.

"Listen!" someone called out. "They're coming!"

The sound of an approaching siren brought murmurs from the people gathered in the parking lot. Within another minute, EMS 1 was parked near the huddled group, and Denton Roberts, the lead paramedic, was out of the ambulance and kneeling beside Jason Best.

"Here, let me take over," he told the fatiguing pediatrician.

With obvious relief, Jason leaned back on his heels and got out of the paramedic's way. He told Denton what he knew and what he had been doing.

"Good work," Denton told him while his partner set up the defibrillator, holding the paddles over Barry's bare chest.

Denton stopped his compressions, and his partner pressed the paddles on bare skin. The two paramedics studied the machine's screen. Nothing. Flatline.

"Jump-start him!" someone yelled from the sidewalk.

The paramedic moved the paddles aside and Denton resumed his compressions.

"There's nothing to shock," Edith Gettys told the would-be cardiologist. "Nothing. Just leave them be."

The two paramedics worked feverishly, continuing chest compressions, securing Barry's airway with an endotracheal tube, starting an IV, and administering emergency cardiac medications.

Minutes passed, and an eerie hush fell over the gathered crowd. Several cars drove into the rest area, drew near the frenzied scene, and then with gawking gazes accelerated further into the parking lot.

Jason Best put his hand on Jane's shoulder. "Let's step over here, out of the way."

He gently guided her to the back of her SUV, followed by his wife and two teenage children. Edith Gettys walked over and put her arm around Jane's waist.

"I think we need to pray," Jason said quietly. "If that's okay with you?"

Jane trembled, her face pale and eyes bloodshot. "Yes," she murmured. "Please."

Without a word, the entire Best family encircled Jane and grabbed each other's hands. Edith kept her arm around Jane, reached back, and put her hand on Jason's shoulder. They bowed their heads and stood there—silent—bound together.

"Lord, we know you are sovereign in all things," Jason began. "And all-powerful. We lift this man up to you and ask for his healing." He paused, and when he next spoke, his voice quivered, and he struggled to go on. "We ask for your mercy and claim the promise of your never-ending love for us. We pray this in the name of Jesus the Christ."

They stood there for a few moments, heads bowed, holding each other. People nearby cleared their throats and turned away.

"We need to get him to the hospital," Denton told his partner. "Let them know what we've got and when we should be there."

Denton continued working while his partner radioed the nearest hospital. He looked over at Denton and shook his head.

"What?" Denton glanced over at Jane Weston.

His partner leaned close and whispered in Denton's ear. "They asked how long he had been down, and when I told the ER doc, he said we should probably go ahead and call it."

Sweat was running into Denton's eyes. He stopped compressions just long enough to wipe his face with his shirtsleeve and peer closely at the cardiac monitor. Still nothing.

His partner had pulled the ambulance stretcher nearby, and Denton motioned toward it.

"Let's at least get him loaded and then see what we've got."

The two men placed the lifeless body of Barry Weston onto their stretcher and rolled it 20 feet to the opened back doors of the ambulance.

"On three," Denton directed. "One, two, three."

They lifted Barry into the ambulance and secured the wheels to the floor. Denton checked the monitor once more and felt for the faintest hint of some cardiac activity. He took a deep breath and turned to face Jane Weston and the small group gathered around her. They had followed the stretcher to the ambulance and stood waiting.

Denton stepped close to Jane.

"I'm sorry, but we tried everything and—"

"Denton! Jump in here! He's breathing!"

Denton spun around and stared at his partner. The paramedic had his hand on Barry Weston's neck.

"And he's got a pulse!"

A gasp spread through the crowd and then a scattering of cheers.

Denton vaulted into the back of the ambulance and checked for himself. Barry did have a pulse—faint, but clearly present. And he was taking weak and gasping breaths.

"Start bagging him," Denton told his partner. "And let's get out of here!"

"What does this mean?" Jane asked, reaching for the closing back doors of the ambulance. "What does…"

Jason Best put his arm around her shoulders and supported the nearly collapsing woman. "Your husband is fighting to stay alive. He's not giving up."

The ambulance motor roared to life, and the unit sped away, lights flashing and siren blaring.

"Get in our car," Jason told her. "And let's follow them to the hospital. We're not from around here, so—"

"I'll go with you," Edith Gettys said. "I know where they're headed."

The ER waiting room was crowded and noisy. Jane Weston and the Best family had somehow managed to find a quiet corner and sat huddled together. Edith was still at the sign-in desk, talking with one of the nurses. She said something, and the nurse smiled and nodded before disappearing through a doorway into the ER. Edith walked over to Jane and the Bests.

"I worked with that girl's mother years ago," she told the waiting group. "She's going to let us know something as soon as they can. Right now, Barry is still breathing on his own, and he has a blood pressure. But he's still very sick, Jane. They're about to take him to the cath lab and will know more soon. One of the staff cardiologists has been in to see him and will meet him there."

"The cath lab?" Jane asked. "Are they going to operate?"

"No, I don't think so." Edith patted her arm and tried to calm her. "But they'll do what they think best, I'm sure."

"It's a miracle he made it this far." Jason stared at the floor and shook his head. "I would never have thought—"

"Dr. Best," Jane interrupted. "I haven't had a chance to thank you for everything you did back there. If you hadn't been sitting on that bank with your family, it would all be different."

He looked up into her face. "That's the funny thing." He paused and glanced at his wife. "Angie will tell you, we never stop at the rest areas on the highway. Just something we don't do. We were heading back to Boone from our friends' house at the beach, and Angie pointed to the sign and said, 'Let's stop and take a break.' Seemed like a natural thing to do somehow. The right thing to do."

"You know, I had the same feeling," Edith said. "I just live right down the road and was on my way to Charlotte. It's been such a beautiful day and the sun was shining, and I just found myself pulling off into that rest area. Not sure why, but I didn't think twice."

"That's some kind of coincidence," the Bests' teenage boy said. "I mean, all this coming together and everything."

Jason reached out and laid a hand on the boy's shoulder. "I'm not sure about this being a coincidence, son. Sometimes we—"

"Mrs. Weston?"

All eyes turned to the young ER doctor standing behind them.

Jane jumped to her feet, and Edith slowly stood, draping an arm around the younger woman's shoulder.

"Yes, I'm…How is he? Is he all right? Is he…"

"He's one lucky man, is all I have to say." He pulled up a chair and pointed to the small sofa. "Have a seat, and I'll tell you what's been happening."

From the moment Barry was wheeled into the department, the entire ER team had descended on him. Chest X-ray, labs, EKG, another IV—all within minutes. The staff cardiologist took one look at Barry's EKG and called the cath lab. Ten minutes later, Barry was being rocketed down the hallway to the waiting cardiology department.

"Widow-maker," the ER doctor told them. "Main blood vessel to the heart, and it was 100 percent occluded. Completely blocked."

"That explains the shoulder pain you told us about," Jason Best said to Jane. "It was never coming from his shoulder joint, but from his heart."

"That's right," the ER doctor agreed. "Like I said, he's one lucky man. Dr. Grover put a stent into the LAD—the blocked vessel—and it opened right up. No heart damage at all. His other vessels looked fine, just not that one."

"But it was enough," Edith opined. "Almost too much."

Jane was on the edge of the sofa. "How is he now? Is he awake? Can I talk with him?"

"He's still in cardiology," the doctor explained. "And will be there for a while. But he's breathing and has a great blood pressure, and he's starting to come around."

"Come around?" Jane's eyes widened. "Is he going to…"

"He was without a pulse for…a long time." The ER doctor glanced at Jason Best. "Maybe 30 or 40 minutes. The brain needs…We'll just have to wait and see. Right now though, your husband is moving and responding."

He stood, took a couple of steps away from them, and then turned, facing Jane once more.

"I spoke with Denton Roberts, the paramedic on the scene. He told me that Doctor Best did a great job with your husband—as did Ms. Gettys." He nodded at both of them. "Quite a coincidence, both of them being at that rest area when your husband collapsed. Quite a coincidence."

He turned again and walked away.

Jane missed her oncology appointment that day. But a week later, she was given great news. Her latest scans and blood work were fine, and her treatments were working. A tough road lay ahead, but she was responding, and there was a reason for hope. Always a reason for hope.

Barry Weston was home from the hospital and recovering from his rest area adventure. He wanted to make the trip to Boone to visit Doctor Best—the man who had saved his life and whom he had never met. That would have to wait for a couple of weeks. His cardiologist was keeping a short leash on him and didn't want him traveling yet.

Edith Gettys had visited a couple of times and had made an unexpected connection. Her sister, a longtime schoolteacher in the area, had taught Barry in junior high school.

"She said you were a good student," Edith told him. "But not necessarily the best behaved."

"Guilty," Barry laughed.

Jane had walked her to the door.

"How's he doing?" Edith whispered. "Apart from his heart?"

Jane smiled. "He's doing great and should be able to go back to work in a few weeks. Of course, he doesn't remember anything from that afternoon, and there are occasional memory lapses. But I think those are *selective*."

"A miracle." Edith chuckled.

They hugged, and Edith stepped outside. Jane closed the door behind her.

Edith stood on the porch for a moment. The sunshine was warm on her face, and she closed her eyes.

"Thank you, Lord."

I truly believe we can either see the connections,
celebrate them, and express gratitude for our blessings,
or we can see life as a string of coincidences
that have no meaning or connection.
For me, I'm going to believe in miracles, celebrate life,
rejoice in the views of eternity,
and hope my choices will create a positive ripple effect
in the lives of others. This is my choice.

MIKE ERICKSEN

10

Big Stan

8:25 p.m.

Amy Connors was filing papers and didn't look up when I slumped into the chair beside her.

"Good to have a little break," the ER unit secretary said. "Been busy all day."

"That bus wreck out on Heckle didn't help," I agreed. "Good thing nobody was hurt, and a good thing Stan was here to help us maintain order."

Amy looked up from her work. "Well, speak of the devil."

A hulk of a man ambled over to the nurses' station and leaned on the counter, right in front of Amy.

"I resemble that remark." Stan Perinsky's voice was deep and booming. He stood six and a half feet tall and weighed a lean 250 pounds.

"We were just remarking that it was a good thing you were working today," I said to the hospital security guard. "The waiting room must have been crazy with all the parents of those kids."

"Not just parents—grandparents, aunts, uncles, cousins, and a bunch of people who didn't have anything better to do. I understand their concern though. If my child had been in a school bus accident—"

"A fender bender," Amy interrupted. "And barely that."

"Still," Stan continued, "if my child had been involved, I'd want to be sure they were okay. But yes, it was crazy out there, Doc."

Stan Perinsky was in his late thirties and famous in these parts. He had been a five-star college football prospect at one of the local high schools, and from his defensive-end position had destroyed every offense he faced. That was until his right knee was blown out by a cheap crackback block from an opposing wide receiver. His surgery was successful, but questions remained, and the piles of scholarship offers dried up and disappeared.

He had taken his misfortune in good stride, as he did with everything that came his way. Stan continued his daily workouts, strengthened that knee, and planned for the next phase of his life.

His path took an interesting turn when he decided to go into law enforcement. His uncle had served on the Rock Hill police force for more than 20 years and had thought Stan would follow in his footsteps. When Stan announced his decision to pursue a career in prison security, his uncle realized the family's "blue line" was going to be broken.

"Jail guard…Is that really what you want to be?"

For Stan it was a higher calling. One of his high school teammates had made several bad choices after graduation and now resided in the "big house" in Columbia. Stan thought he could make a difference, and his uncle's disdain didn't dissuade him.

Ten years and several advancements as a prison guard proved to be enough, and Stan decided on another career change. Hospital security. His uncle was gone now, but Stan could imagine his response.

"What? A hospital rent-a-cop? When are you going to get a real job?"

Stan knew this was a real job, and an important one. He had several friends on the hospital staff—techs, nurses, and a couple of physicians who were parents of his high school teammates. He was convinced he would like the environment, especially the ER, where "something is always going on."

We were happy with his decision. His mere physical presence was often enough to quell any incipient uprising in the department, the waiting room, or the parking lot. The ER staff had enough to do taking care of patients without worrying about their safety or our own.

Stan had been on the job less than two weeks when we realized just how important his decision to join us had been and what a valuable addition he was to our team.

EMS 1 had brought a stab wound into Major Trauma, the victim of a family outing gone wrong. Several cousins had gotten into an argument over some girl…or maybe it was a football game. Didn't matter, because knives were quickly drawn and waved around, and someone got cut. Then someone got stabbed. Onlookers called 911, and EMS arrived on the scene moments after a police cruiser. The paramedics were happy for that circumstance. The backyard was a chaotic mess, with men yelling, women screaming, and neighborhood kids peering out of windows and over the wooden and crumbling fence.

The paramedics were able to locate the victim, get him on a stretcher, and get out of there before something else happened.

They wheeled their patient through the ambulance doors and straight to Trauma. Five minutes later, we heard yelling and screaming from the waiting room—and then what sounded like a chair being thrown against a wall.

One of the secretaries ran through the triage entrance, wide-eyed and screaming, "We need security! We need security!"

She disappeared down the hallway as Amy Connors paged overhead.

Before she could put the phone back into its cradle, two men bolted through the triage door and into the department. They were both barefoot, both wore dirty blue jeans and nappy T-shirts, and both held knives. One of the blades was an evil-looking hawkbill, its holder intent upon mayhem.

"Where is he?" one of the men yelled. "Where did they take him?"

One of the paramedics from EMS 1 stepped out of Major Trauma and froze in the hallway.

"There!" one of the men yelled, taking a couple of steps in the paramedic's direction. "He's in there!"

The paramedic took a step back as the men approached, waving their weapons.

"If you're looking for me, I'm right here."

The voice was low, ominous, and coming from behind them.

The men stopped and spun around.

"That's right—I'm right here."

Stan Perinsky had been patrolling the parking lot and heard the commotion. Without a sound, he walked into the department through the ambulance entrance and now stood in front of the nurses' station, glowering at the intruders.

They stole quick glances at each other and then, as if on cue, changed their knives from one hand to the other and back again.

Stan had no weapon in his hand and only a radio on his black leather belt. But his eyes were piercing and his muscled body tense. He was ready.

Painful and absolute silence. The three men stared at each other without a word.

Stan's threatening voice broke the hushed standoff.

"Guys, we can do this one of two ways. And you get to choose."

They stared at him for a moment and then glanced around the department. Again, as if on cue, they dropped their knives and ran back through the triage entrance and into the night.

Even the walls of the ER uttered a loud and grateful sigh of relief.

There would be other occasions when Stan came riding to the rescue, but that first instance carved out his place in the department, and he became one of us.

"Yeah, glad those kids are okay," Stan said. "The only real problem I had was with three irate parents whose kids weren't even on the bus. Go figure that one out."

"Yeah, go figure," Amy offered. "Just goes to show how goofy some people can be."

"You're not talking about *me* being goofy again, are you?"

Matt Jenkins, our newest and youngest partner, strolled up to the desk and dropped the chart of room 3 on the counter.

"No, not goofy," Amy grinned at him. "Just wet behind the ears."

Matt looked barely old enough to have finished college, but he had graduated from medical school at Duke and completed a residency in emergency medicine in Atlanta. He was well trained, but Amy was right. He was still a little wet behind the ears.

He made some notes on the chart in front of him and slid it across the counter to Amy.

"We'll need some labs and a chest X-ray in 3." He looked at me and nodded. "Probable pneumonia. We'll see."

Matt picked up the chart of another of his patients. He looked at it for a moment and then put it back on the counter. Turning to Stan he said, "I want to thank you again for your help the other night. I had no clue what was going on. Just glad you were here."

Amy cocked her head. "What's this about? You found yourself in a jam or something?"

"Yeah, Matt," I followed. "What are you talking about?"

"Nothing," Stan said, straightening and stepping back from the counter.

"Hold on there," I told him. "You're not going anywhere until you tell us what Matt is talking about."

"I'll tell you," the young ER doctor interjected. "But don't you go anywhere, Stan."

Two weeks earlier, Matt Jenkins had been on duty in the ER—the graveyard shift. A little after three in the morning, two sheriff's deputies brought in a 20-year-old man they had found in the middle of Highway 161. He was naked except for a pair of purple, silk drawers—and they were on backward.

The officers held the slender young man between them, each clutching one of his arms to their chest.

"Got a wild one here, Doc. Where do you want him?"

Lori Davidson, the nurse on duty, walked over and asked, "Do we have any idea what's going on with him? Any trauma or alcohol? What about drugs? And what's his name?"

She motioned the group to follow her into the Cardiac room. It was empty, large, and close to the nurses' station.

"Bubba is all he will tell us," one of the deputies said. "Doubt that's his name, but that's all we've got."

"That's me! Bubba!"

The young man managed to get one arm free and proceeded to whip it in the air, striking one of the deputies several times in the face.

"I told you about that!" the deputy shouted. He grabbed Bubba's arm, wrenching it behind his back.

"Oooo! That hurts so good!"

"Get him in here on the stretcher," Lori told them.

A few minutes later, Bubba was resting quietly on the bed with his arms and legs securely restrained in rolled-up sheets. The two deputies stood by his side—their chests heaving from the exertion and sweat dripping from their faces.

Matt walked into the room. "What have you got so far, Lori?"

He walked over to the man and put an open palm on his chest.

"He's cool," he observed. "What's his temp?"

Lori answered, "Checked it twice—95. And his heart rate is 120."

"Don't know why he would be cool," one of the deputies said. "Except he's only in his underwear. But it's warm outside—still around 75 or so. And the way he was jumpin' all around..."

"Blood pressure's elevated too," Lori told him. "I'll get a line started and get him on a monitor."

"We'll need some labs too, and probably a drug screen," Matt said. "But that won't be back in time to do us any good."

He took his hand off Bubba's chest and gently raised one of the man's eyelids. The size of his pupil was normal, and it reacted normally to the light in the room. A quick exam didn't reveal any evidence of trauma, and there was no white, powdery residue in his nose.

"Anything at the scene? Any needles or anything like that?"

"Doc, we were standing in the middle of the highway, so we didn't have much time to look around. Just a cigarette in his hand that we made him put out. Nothing else."

"A cigarette? You mean a joint?" Matt leaned close and smelled Bubba's face and hair.

"Marijuana?" the deputy asked. "Could have been, but it was dark, and we were just trying to get him out of the road. He was lookin' up in the sky and mumbling something about spaceships and cows and stuff. You want us to go back and check?"

Matt rubbed his chin.

"No, probably blown away by now. He seems to be calming down and we'll—"

"Yeow!"

Bubba arched his back and jerked his arms and legs. He twisted from side to side with wild eyes and a blank stare.

"Yeow!"

"Do we need to sedate him?" Lori reached for the emergency drug cart and pulled it close to the stretcher.

Before Matt could say anything, Bubba relaxed and closed his eyes.

"You think it's PCP, Doc?" one of the officers asked. "We had a guy not too long ago that was standing in the middle of Celanese Road with a red cape, bullfighting the cars that came by. But he was *completely* naked. Turned out to be PCP—just sayin'."

"Something to think about," Matt muttered. "Some strange things here though. Low temperature but high blood pressure and heart rate. Normal pupils. It doesn't make sense."

He turned toward the door and took a few steps toward the nurses' station. The metal rails of the stretcher clanged together, and the entire bed seemed to be bouncing off the floor. Matt spun around. Bubba was seizing—a full-blown grand mal. Saliva foamed from his mouth, and his arms and legs shook with violent tremors. The deputies, wide-eyed now, backed away from the stretcher and pressed themselves against the wall.

"Four milligrams of lorazepam IV!" Matt called out. "And have some more ready if that doesn't do it."

It took the lorazepam and a couple of other drugs to get Bubba's seizures under control. His body was exhausted, as were Lori and Matt. The deputies had disappeared, and when Matt turned to the door, Stan Perinsky was standing there, almost filling the entire frame.

"What ya got, Doc?"

"Beats me, Stan. I don't know of anything that causes all the stuff we're seeing here. I'm at a loss."

Stan moved out of the doorway, and Matt walked to the nurses' station. He stood there, grimacing and rubbing his temples.

Stan stood behind him and said, "Spice."

Matt's hands froze, and he turned around. "What? Spice?"

"Yeah, you know—Spice, K2. Synthetic marijuana. I've seen it do this kind of stuff a bunch of times."

"Spice…" Matt repeated. "I seem to remember something…"

He rushed around the counter and sat down behind one of the computer screens. A toxicology database gave him the answer. Actually, Big Stan had given him the answer. The website just confirmed it.

"That's it, Stan! You're right. Thanks."

"Spice," I murmured. "I've only seen one or two cases, and it's been a couple of years. Used to be able to get the stuff online and in head shops, but not anymore. But that wouldn't have been my first thought. How did you come up with the answer, Stan?"

"Ten years as a prison guard, Doc. I've seen just about everything there is to see. All kinds of violence, for sure. But also overdoses. You name it, we've got it in prison."

"How does that happen?" I leaned forward in my chair. "How does an inmate get hold of something that would cause an overdose? And Spice? How would they get *that* in prison?"

"Doc, you can get everything you want in prison. It's all about money and determination. Where there's a will, there's a way."

"I thought prisons X-rayed everything that came in." Amy rolled her chair back and looked up at Stan. "Like in the movies when people would smuggle knives and stuff in brownies."

"Don't need to smuggle knives into prison," Stan answered. "Just make your own out of toilet paper."

"What?" Matt stared at him. "Toilet paper into a knife? You've got to be kidding."

"Don't try this at home, but it's really pretty simple," Stan began to explain. "You take some toilet paper, wet it, twist it into the shape of a knife, and let it dry. Then you add more toilet paper and do it again and again."

"Just like papier-mâché," I volunteered.

"Yeah, but it takes a lot longer—a little at a time. You have to keep at it until it's rock-solid and sharp. And then you've got your shank or shiv—whatever you want to call it."

"Takes some patience *and* time," Amy said.

"That's all they've got—time," Stan agreed. "But like I said, it's all about the money. If you can get a cigarette smuggled in, it's worth $20."

"Twenty bucks?" Amy was incredulous. "That's crazy."

"And a cell phone—that'll cost you a thousand."

"Wait a minute," I chimed in. "A cell phone? How would you go about getting one of those in prison?"

"Friends, money, and opportunity," Stan told us. "There's always an opportunity. And the thousand is just for a flip phone. A smartphone will cost you two thousand."

"But what good is a cell phone without a charger?" Matt was thinking ahead.

"That will be three thousand."

"Wait, go back a minute," I interrupted. "How would you go about getting a phone and a charger into a prison?"

"Lots of ways. You just have to use your imagination. One of the best I ever saw was in a facility in the lower part of the state. The warden had decided to do some extensive painting, and a big shipment of paint cans came in early one morning. Pallets full of sealed cans and the whole thing wrapped in plastic. Who would have been suspicious? But somebody got mad at somebody else and passed the word that they needed to X-ray those cans."

"See, I told you," Amy beamed. "X-rays. I'd X-ray everything."

"Well, they did," Stan continued. "And when they finished X-raying all those paint cans, they found more than a hundred chargers and a couple hundred smartphones. Somebody was going to make a lot of money."

"Bet there were some upset people," Matt added. "In and out of prison."

"You're right about that, Dr. Jenkins. We had some strange injuries after the paint business."

"Let's get back to the Spice business, Stan," I said. "How do you know so much about synthetic marijuana?"

"It's been a few years, but that stuff was all the rage for a while— especially in prison. We'd see a couple of guys each week spaced out with the stuff. And one guy I remember almost died. I was on duty in the common area—minding my own business—when one of the inmates comes walking over. Not walking so much as listing from side to side, shuffling his feet and mumbling stuff I couldn't understand. I knew he was on something when he crossed the red line."

"Wait a minute," I interrupted. "What's the red line?"

"It's a stripe of red paint—a circle or box—that surrounds the officer on duty. Every inmate knows not to cross that line or it's big trouble. This guy kept lurching toward me with a wild look in his eyes. I told him to stop, but he wouldn't listen—or couldn't listen. He crossed the line, and I was about to grab him when he jerked straight up, fell over, and started seizing. That went on for more than an hour, even after the prison medical people had given him a ton of medicine. I thought his brain was fried when he left in an ambulance, but two weeks later, he was back. Never quite the same though. Not as sharp, not as talkative. And he always shuffled a little. That Spice stuff is bad news."

"How did he get hold of it?" Amy asked.

"It's like I said—imagination," Stan explained. "The guys would play handball outside, using the side of the building as a backstop. Somebody had some friends who would slip up in the woods just outside the outer fence and lob a handball between the outer and inner fences—just out of reach of the guys playing. One of the inmates would pocket the ball, call a guard, and point to the ball that had been thrown over. He'd tell them they'd accidentally knocked it over the fence and ask them to get it. When they did, it was a simple thing to change it out, go back inside, and empty the contents. That's how this guy got his Spice—inside a handball."

"How did they go about stopping that?" Matt asked.

"Well," Stan chuckled, "you won't see any trees around that prison for a couple hundred yards. But they'll find another way—always do. Like I said, where there's a will, there's a way."

"And where there's money," I added.

"Anyway," Matt said. He picked up his chart again and looked at Stan. "I'm just glad you were here that night and came to the rescue. I really needed your help."

"Think nothing of it, Doctor Jenkins." Big Stan grinned and nodded. "Anytime you need help, just call me."

The best way to find yourself
is to lose yourself in the service of others.

MAHATMA GANDHI

11

It's Not Always Black-and-White

So this is how it happens—how a man's true character and the hidden condition of his heart are exposed.

October 31, 11:45 p.m.

Jeff Ryan was the triage nurse on duty in the ER. The waiting room was empty, and he walked to the nurses' station and plopped into a chair beside Amy Connors.

"Pretty tame for a Halloween." He leaned back in the chair and folded his hands behind his head.

"Shh! You'll jinx us," Amy chided. "Now it'll all break loose. Just you wait."

I leaned on the counter and glanced around the empty department—unusual for *any* night.

"I think we've weathered the storm," I told them. "All the trick-or-treaters are home and probably stuffing their faces, or they have upset stomachs and wish they hadn't."

"Probably the latter," Jeff said. "Hasn't always been like this though. I remember when Halloween was one of the busiest nights in the ER—and for EMS. Don't know why, but that seems to have changed over the last ten or fifteen years."

"You're right," Amy agreed. "Maybe more people stay at home now than they did back in the day. We'd see all kinds of stuff—grown adults getting into fights over their kids' costumes, people walkin' into stuff in the dark, and that guy who dressed up like a scarecrow and sat real still on his front porch. When kids would come up, he'd jump up and scare them—until one six-year-old grabbed a hoe handle and whacked him on the head. What was that, about 20 stitches?

"And remember when we had parents bring their kids' candy in to be X-rayed? One year there was a big scare when a razor blade was found in some chocolate candy or something. Not sure where that happened, but it was all in the news, and everybody panicked and came to the ER."

"Yeah, the hospital put out some notice that we'd X-ray candy just to be sure it was safe," Jeff added. "I don't know who made that deci-sion—guess they thought it would be good PR. Turned out to be a PR nightmare."

Amy chuckled and shook her head. "I remember we had a five-year-old boy who broke his arm and was about to go to radiology to have it X-rayed. A pile of people stormed into the department and demanded their kids' candy be X-rayed right then and there, before anybody else. You had us call security, Doc. Remember that?"

"Yeah, I remember that all too well. Trying to take care of patients in the midst of all that chaos. And we had to look at all those X-rays because the radiologists had already gone home."

"Probably out trick-or-treating themselves," Amy jested.

"Had never seen so many Twinkies and Tootsie Pops and M&M's—before or since," I lamented.

"Did anything ever turn up?" Jeff looked over at me. "Anything sus-picious or dangerous?"

"Well, we did find the back of an earring in a candy apple. Some mother had been making them when her earring came off. She was sure it was somewhere in the caramel, and she brought two dozen of them in to be X-rayed. Turns out it wasn't *in* the apple itself, just sitting there in the wrapper. She was happy about that."

"So let's see—about a hundred X-rays and one piece of an earring," Amy smiled. "Lots of impatient and upset people and no charges for the hospital. Bet the administrator wasn't very happy about that."

"I don't think anybody was happy about that night." I shook my head. "That was the one and only Halloween we ever offered free X-rays for candy."

"And a good thing too." Amy rolled her chair back and looked up at me. "Speaking of crazy things—you remember that Halloween 10 or 15 years ago and Bucky Watts?"

"Bucky Watts," I repeated slowly, searching my memory banks. A face flashed before me, and there he was. "You mean the little tow-headed boy with a penchant for pennies?"

"That's the one. Bucky Watts."

Halloween 1989

The ambulance doors opened and EMS rolled their stretcher into the department and up to the nurses' station. On it perched Frances Watts, a thirty-year-old woman dressed in blue jeans and a Clemson sweatshirt. In her lap sat her toddler, Bucky. He was two and a half.

"What happened this time?" I asked Frances.

"It's bad." Her voice was low and troubled. "Real bad."

We all knew Bucky on a first-name basis. Since turning two, he had been a visitor to the ER on at least a half-dozen occasions. Once or twice it had been for fever and maybe an ear infection. On all the other occasions, it was because of his ingestion of a coin—sometimes several. He seemed to have a preference for pennies, but a nickel or a dime would do. Any coin he found on the floor or on a table within his reach was fair game. He hadn't located a quarter yet, whose size might be problematic. And thank heaven his parents didn't leave silver dollars lying around. But every time his mother thought he had swallowed a coin, she had been right. We were obliged to get a "kiddiegram"— a single, low exposure X-ray of his chest and abdomen. A coin will block the X-rays from reaching the film, preventing any "exposure" and resulting in a round, white spot. Air, on the other hand, allows the X-rays to cleanly strike the film, exposing it and turning it black. Quite a contrast, allowing for a quick assessment and location of a metallic foreign body. Black-and-white.

On one of these occasions, I pointed to three perfectly round objects in Bucky's stomach. Upon close inspection—and with a little imagination—the Lincoln Memorial could just barely be visualized on one of them.

"Looks like he managed to swallow three pennies," I told Frances. "They're in his stomach and should pass without any problems."

"But what I am supposed to do?"

"Just watch for any change in his stool."

That worked once. After that, she was quick to remind me not to make that smart-aleck remark ever again.

"What's the problem tonight?" I asked Frances. "More coins?"

"No, it's worse than that, Dr. Lesslie. I can't find my car keys, and I just know Bucky has swallowed them."

Amy looked up from behind the counter and stared—first at the boy and then at me.

"Car keys?" I asked Frances. That was *plural* and could be a problem.

"Yes, three of them on a small chain. That's why we had to come in by ambulance. I only have one set and can't start the car."

I looked at Bucky and was met by his large, brown eyes. He was calm, breathing quietly, and not drooling—all good signs that he didn't have something stuck in his airway or upper esophagus.

But Frances had always been right, and if Bucky had swallowed three keys, it wasn't likely that he would be able to pass them. And she was right about this being bad.

"Let's get an X-ray and see what we have."

About 30 minutes later, the X-ray tech dropped Bucky's kiddiegram on the counter and shook her head. I picked it up, walked over to the X-ray view box, and snapped the film into place over the lighted surface. There was the answer. Three keys on a small chain, sitting somewhere in his lower stomach or upper small intestine—a tangled metal mess. There was no way he was going to be able to pass these. We would need to call a surgeon.

I had my finger on the light switch when something caught my eye. I peered closer at the X-ray, shifting my head from side to side.

I flipped off the light and walked over to room 4. Francis was standing silently by the stretcher. Bucky was lying quietly, the sheet drawn up to his neck. I pulled it down, exposing his chest and then his belly.

The X-ray tech was still standing at the nurses' station, talking with Amy. I motioned her over.

"Did you take Bucky's X-ray with all his clothes off?" That would be the standard procedure.

She glanced down at the boy and shook her head. "We got his shirt off, but when we tried to slip off his pants, he went crazy. We gave up and just shot the film."

Bucky looked up at us, bare-chested. He wore some loose-fitting jeans—zipperless—with three or four buttons fastening them in the front.

That's what had caught my eye on his X-ray. Barely visible, these buttons had created faint shadows on the X-ray. I had almost missed them, and now I knew what had happened.

"Should we make another X-ray?" the tech asked. "It will only take a few minutes."

I shook my head and patted the front pockets of Bucky's jeans. Nothing. Gently, I slid a hand under him and checked the two rear pockets. The left was flat, empty. The right…

I stood and dangled the three missing keys, raised my eyebrows, and smiled at Bucky Watts. He would be heading home and not to the OR.

"Well I'll be," Frances muttered. "Imagine that."

"Wasn't it just a year later that they brought in Tim Stanley? Came in around midnight, I think. On Halloween."

Jeff and I looked at Amy. As if a switch somewhere had been flipped, the mood of the entire room changed. A somber, leaden cloud descended over our pained silence.

"We need help here! Officer shot!"

Everyone in the department turned their heads in the direction of the ambulance entrance, its doors flung open by a crowd of police officers. They raced into the ER, carrying the limp body of another officer. The young man's head flopped from side to side, and blood dripped from his saturated shirt and pants, splashing on the tiled floor.

"Major Trauma!" Lori Davidson rushed ahead of them down the hall and into Trauma. She motioned one of the other nurses to join her, flipped on the light switch, and pointed to the stretcher. "Put him down there."

Sergeant Woodward walked to the nurses' station and grabbed my arm.

"That's Tim Stanley." His face was flushed and sweaty. "Shot twice in the belly at close range, just below his vest. No pulse at the scene—and a lot of blood. I don't think…"

He avoided my eyes and stared at the countertop. Turning, he nodded at an officer standing by the triage entrance. He was motionless, pale, and staring at the group disappearing into Major Trauma—unseeing.

"That's his partner, JT Anderson."

Ten units of blood and two hours later, Officer Tim Stanley was pronounced dead in the operating room. His wife and three-year-old boy, along with Sergeant Woodward, were in the ER family room. I tapped on the door and stepped in.

Tim and his partner, JT Anderson, had responded a few hours earlier to a "possible breaking and entering" on Gulledge Avenue, a dead-end street in what had once been a respectable part of town. The area had fallen into disrepair and now had the reputation of being a good source for whatever drugs you fancied and a wide variety of other illicit activities.

There remained a few rare pockets of hardworking and responsible people, among whom was Sally Green. She had worked for years in the local school district and was determined to stay in the white clapboard two-story house she had grown up in. Every Halloween, her porch was crowded with ghosts and fairies and clowns, each clamoring for what was always the best stash of candy for blocks around.

This Halloween had been no different. By ten o'clock, the throng of costumed children had thinned, and when there came a knock on the door—heavier and louder than any preceding it—she was surprised.

Sally picked up the bowl of candy from the table beside the entrance and opened the front door.

Three men stood on the porch, each wearing what might have passed for the Lone Ranger's mask. Not much of a disguise, and she immediately recognized one of the two African-Americans.

"Jarad Bascom, what are you doing out here trick-or-treating with all these young folks?"

The lone white male had been facing the sidewalk, his head turning from side to side, apparently scanning the street. He spun around and bolted through the door, grabbed Sally by her throat, and threw her down on a nearby sofa.

"Don't make a sound," he threatened in her ear.

Sally was almost 80 and not strong enough to resist her assailant.

"Jarad," she croaked, looking over the man's shoulder toward Bascom. "What are you doing?"

"Shut up!" Jarad yelled. He slammed the door and headed to the back of the house. "Where do you keep your money? I know you've got some here. Where is it?"

The grip on her throat tightened, and she closed her eyes, unable to speak.

"Mike, make sure she doesn't make any noise," Jarad told the man holding Sally. "Dez and I are going to check the house."

Mike couldn't know, but in spite of his attempted surveillance on the front porch, a neighbor had seen the three men enter the house and immediately called 911. Tim Stanley and JT Anderson were already en route, lights flashing and siren blaring.

A few minutes passed, and Mike heard the approaching police. "Jarad! We've got to get out of here! The cops are coming!"

Jarad and his partner ran wide-eyed into the living room.

Mike released his grip on Sally's throat and took a few steps toward the back of the house.

"Not that way," Jarad said. He knew the house and neighborhood— a high fence in the rear of the property would prevent their escape. "Out the front door, quick!"

Blue flashing lights reflected off the living room windows as they opened the door and burst onto the front porch.

"Hold it right there!" Tim Stanley was standing on the sidewalk, flashlight and service weapon pointed at the three men. JT was steps behind. "Don't move," Tim again warned the three men.

Mike jumped off one side of the porch into some dense bushes, and Dez did the same on the other side. Jarad stood alone on the porch.

"Don't move," Tim repeated. "Let me see your hands."

Jarad reached behind him and grabbed a handgun.

Shots rang out, and Jarad's limp body fell on the porch.

Tim dropped to his knees on the sidewalk and then slumped to the ground.

"Officer down," JT yelled into his radio. "Officer down. We need EMS and backup!"

Moments later, Tim Stanley was on his way to the ER. Mike Tolbert and Desmond Waters had been apprehended in a nearby alley, and Jarad Bascom was sitting on Sally Green's front porch. He pressed several pieces of cotton gauze to the grazing wound on the left side of his head—superficial, and needing only the attention of the paramedics on the scene. He was cuffed, surrounded by several police officers, and would soon be heading to the jail and a quick conviction.

Jarad Bascom had a good attorney and a confused jury. His sentence of 15 years had been met with outrage by Tim's family, by most in the community, and by all of the police force. The ensuing years only partially blunted those emotions, and when he was released, there was a legitimate concern for his safety. He didn't come back to Rock Hill but seemed to drop off the face of the earth.

Until October 2015. Jarad Bascom was back in town but trying to lay low—at least according to some of his friends. He had been somewhere in Florida, ran out of money, had some trouble with the law, and decided to head home. He was staying with his aunt and working a few odd jobs—just enough to cover the cost of his Rock and Rye whiskey.

JT Anderson had never gotten over the death of his partner, and a deep-seated bitterness gnawed at his heart. He blamed himself for not being quicker, for not getting a shot off before Jarad Bascom, and even for being the one who was still alive. But mainly he blamed Bascom and his careless disdain for life that would allow him to use a handgun without thinking, without remorse. And for what? A few dollars that Sally Green might have hidden away somewhere?

That Halloween night had changed JT Anderson, bent his spirit, and wouldn't let him go. Sergeant Woodward had seen the change and had talked with JT on a number of occasions. The younger man seemed to listen, but Woodward was worried. According to his fellow officers, JT was always the first to rush into a dangerous situation, subduing suspects with quickness and strength. Never excessive, but he was always ready to do what needed to be done. But that was not all that troubled Woodward.

Jarad Bascom had been black, and JT was white. When Woodward heard that race might be becoming a factor in how Anderson approached certain circumstances, he took action. Nothing definite had surfaced, and any off-the-record statement always started with "I wonder if…" Still, Woodward wasn't going to wait for something to explode. JT was too good an officer, and the department had worked too hard and too long to maintain good race relations in the community.

"JT, we're going to change things up a little bit," Sergeant Woodward told the officer one morning. "Starting tomorrow, Pete Carson is going to be your new partner."

It wasn't unusual for these things to happen. Just like the coach of a football team, Woodward was always looking for the right combination of officers, pairing different sets of skills and strengths. JT must have assumed this was the case, and he accepted the sergeant's decision with no complaints. It didn't seem to matter that Corporal Pete Carson was black.

Pete had been with the force for more than 20 years and was one of its best officers. He had the uncanny and uncommon knack for defusing the most volatile situations with his size, his strength, and his warm and genuine smile. Woodward had shared his concerns with Pete regarding JT, and the corporal had simply smiled, nodded, and said, "I'll handle it."

Three months after this new partnership had been forged, the two officers found themselves patrolling Cherry Road when the call came in.

"Disabled vehicle on I-77—northbound on the Catawba River Bridge. Blocking traffic."

Pete was driving, and he executed a smooth U-turn as JT told Dispatch they were minutes away and would handle the call.

It was two a.m. with little traffic on Cherry, and only a few vehicles on the interstate. With lights flashing, they exited Cherry onto the ramp and within a few minutes were approaching the bridge.

"That must be it." JT pointed to an Oldsmobile wagon parked at an odd angle on the right side of the highway. It had stopped at the highest point of the bridge, more than a hundred feet above the slow-moving water. Its nose was up against the rail, and its dented rear was sitting in the right-hand lane.

Pete slowed the patrol car and pulled up behind the stranded vehicle. "Better call for a wrecker," he said. "I'll handle traffic. How about checking on the car and seeing if anyone's inside? Doesn't look like an accident. More like somebody pulled over and—look, JT! On the other side of the car!"

JT opened his door and stepped out onto the concrete shoulder. It was narrow—only about five feet wide—and bordered by a three-foot-high cement wall topped with a low metal rail. JT directed the beam of his flashlight to the front of the Oldsmobile. It came to rest on the figure of a man standing on the other side of the rail, somehow finding a foothold on what must have been a narrow ledge. One of his hands gripped the rail and the other was waving wildly in the air.

Two cars approached them, heading north.

"I'll take care of this," Pete said, stepping to the rear of the patrol car and waving his flashlight in the direction of the rapidly nearing cars. "Looks like we might have a jumper. See if you can get him down from there. Nothing but shallow rocks and bad news."

JT took a few steps toward the man, trying to be as quiet as possible. He didn't seem to be aware of their presence, and JT wanted to get as close to the man as he could before he was detected.

One of the approaching cars sped by Pete and was gone. The other slowed, and the driver starting blowing his horn.

The man by the rail spun his head around and looked straight at JT Anderson. The officer's flashlight shone directly into his face.

JT flushed, and his hand holding the flashlight trembled.

Jarad Bascom.

A look of recognition spread across Jarad's face, and then a drunken, leering smile. He turned his head and stared down at the black water below.

JT looked at Pete, and their eyes locked. Pete had seen the man's face and knew it was Jarad Bascom. He knew the story, and he remembered how angry he had been when Tim Stanley had been killed. And he knew how devastated JT had been.

Pete took a step toward the two men and called out JT's name. Anderson was now staring at Bascom—unmoving, waiting.

"JT!" Pete called out again.

Too late. With a wild "Whoop!" Jarad jumped off the side of the bridge and disappeared.

To this day, Pete Carson still doesn't know how it happened. JT seemed to fly from where he stood, reached over the rail, and grabbed Jarad's arm. The officer's body was pressed against the rail, straining to maintain a grip on Jarad and on the rail beneath him. He wasn't about to drop the man, but he was losing his fight with the rail and with gravity and was inching over the side. Both men were going to die.

Pete dropped his flashlight, raced to his partner, wrapped his arms around his waist, and somehow pulled both men to safety.

Jarad lay on the side of the highway, mumbling incoherently but alive.

Exhausted and gasping, the two officers stood and stared at each other. Finally Pete nodded and smiled.

Sometimes it *is* black-and-white.

Do not repay evil with evil or insult with insult.
On the contrary, repay evil with blessing,
because to this you were called
so that you may inherit a blessing.

1 PETER 3:9

12

Into the Storm

O kay, who's got the Fourth of July?"

Fire Chief Nate Pritchard stood at the front of the call room, surveying the crews under his command.

Captain Shep Stevens raised his hand and glanced around at his team. They had drawn the short straw and with it, the holiday duty on Lake McDowell. It promised to be a long, hot day with probably nothing more exciting than towing a couple of broken-down boats back to shore or breaking up a teenage keg party.

"Good." Pritchard nodded and made a note on the pad of paper in his hand. "Just keep in mind the trouble we had last year. And there will probably be a lot more boats on the water this holiday—and more alcohol."

"Got it, Chief," Shep responded. "We'll be sure to stay visible."

Shep and his crew would be on Fireboat 23 assigned to the lake. Normally they manned one of the heavy rescue engines, but on Labor Day, Memorial Day, and the Fourth of July, the department's presence was needed on the largest and busiest lake in the area.

In addition to Captain Stevens, the crew included Engineer Roddy Langston, Firefighter Troy Adams, and Firefighter Lanny Woods. They had been together for more than eight years and, in the words of Langston, functioned like a well-oiled machine.

The Fourth fell on a Saturday this year, which created the potential of a very large crowd on Lake McDowell. The man-made lake stretched more than 15 miles with more than 300 miles of shoreline. Starting where a power company had dammed the Deep River in 1904 to build a hydroelectric plant, it was fed by numerous streams and another upriver power-plant dam. That plant was named Choctaw Springs, and when its water was released to produce electricity, you didn't want to be standing, swimming, or boating within a quarter mile below it.

The morning started quietly enough, and Shep's crew had a chance to drink their coffee, get settled in the covered boat, and take a leisurely run over to Mason's Point. "The Point" was a sandbar that extended a hundred yards from one of the many coves created by the dam and was a favorite spot for afternoon and late-night parties. After heavy rains, the sandbar would disappear and pose a significant hazard for unsuspecting boaters. But there had been little rain so far this summer, and the sandy beach was well above water level and deserted.

"Peaceful now," Troy Adams observed. "But wait till four o'clock or so."

"Take us up to Choctaw," Shep instructed his engineer. "Let's make sure everything's quiet up at that end of the lake."

Roddy Langston adjusted their course, and the crew headed west.

A few boats began making their way onto the lake—mainly early morning fishermen trying to catch something before the crowd descended. Shep waved at a couple of guys he recognized, and they continued up the narrowing waterway.

"You believe in this alligator stuff, Captain?" Troy was leaning over the boat's rail, studying the ripples and eddies created by their passing.

"Do I believe in alligators?" Shep answered, smiling. "Sure. Don't you?"

"You know what I mean," Troy protested. "Alligators here in Lake McDowell. Some people swear they've seen them."

"Usually after a six-pack of Bud Light," Roddy interjected. "Heck, by then you see a lot of stuff out here."

"Too far north, I think," Shep opined. "But I guess anything is possible. Global warming and all that."

"Holy smoke! Look over there!" Lanny Woods was pointing up ahead where the lake meandered past an old pier, turned to their right, and disappeared into a small passage that led to the Choctaw dam. It was a great fishing spot, especially for catfish. But if you didn't know the schedule for water release from the dam, it could be dangerous.

Every crew member turned, and their eyes followed Lanny's finger. Just beyond the pier was a small, plastic boat—sold by a local sporting-goods store and meant to hold one person. Maybe two, if they were both small or were children.

"Would you look at that." Troy shook his head in disbelief.

The boat couldn't have been more than six feet long and only a couple across. Perched in the bow was a large young woman, her hands tightly gripping the sides. She must have heard the approaching fireboat and turned to face them. The slight movement caused the boat to rock, almost throwing her into the water.

She screamed and spun around to face the skipper of this tiny vessel. At the stern was a slender, bare-chested young man who was struggling to control the small trolling motor. He wasn't having much success, and the plastic skiff made slow, sweeping circles in the water.

"Get me out of here!" the young woman yelled at him.

Her captain didn't respond. He gripped the handle of the motor with both hands and stared straight ahead.

"Should we go help them?" Troy asked, chuckling.

As if to answer his question, two things happened.

A loud blast from upstream echoed down the lake, bouncing off the pines crowding each bank. The Choctaw power plant was announcing the discharge of water—a lot of water. It would be making its way in their direction within minutes, and while not exactly a tidal wave, the leading crest could be a foot or so high and moving fast.

The other occurrence was the sudden ability of the skiff's captain to gain control of his trolling motor and rudder. Just as the horn sounded, the plastic boat ceased its circling, straightened its course, and headed straight upstream toward the Choctaw dam.

"You think he knows what that horn means?" Troy asked.

"Doesn't look like it," Shep answered. He motioned his engineer to follow the two star-crossed sailors. "We better go get them."

Too late. From around the next bend, a wave of swirling water was fast approaching.

"Jimmy! What are you doing?" The passenger of the boat was panicking now and screaming.

Jimmy didn't respond. He stood in the boat, precariously perched at the back, and stared at impending disaster. He jerked on the motor's handle, sending the plastic boat into a dizzying spin before finally heading straight toward the fireboat.

Engineer Roddy Langston slowed the motor and adjusted his course, trying not to send the two overboard.

Too late again. The crest of the wave washed over the skiff, and Jimmy was gone. His passenger tried desperately to maintain some sort of balance, but the boat was rocking wildly, and in the blink of an eye, it flipped.

"Susie!" Jimmy had surfaced and saw the boat capsize and his girlfriend disappear beneath the surface. Seconds later, she was thrashing beside him, spewing water and some salty sailor-worthy language.

"Let's get them on board," Shep directed his crew. An opening in one of the side rails allowed a plank-like structure to extend out from the fireboat at water level, making it easy for people to get on board.

Jimmy was the closest, and he scrambled on first. Shep had heard and seen the interaction between the two, and he motioned Troy to guide Jimmy to the back of the boat. A little separation might be in order.

Next came Susie, spluttering and scampering over the landing board. "Where is he!" Her eyes darted around the boat, searching for Jimmy.

"Here, dry yourself off with this." Shep handed her a towel and gently guided her to the front of the boat. "Lanny, let's take them to the pier we passed back there."

The lake was calm again, having adjusted to the inflow of water from above the dam, and the engineer made a wide, sweeping turn and headed away from the scene of this near disaster.

"The boat!" Jimmy yelled. "Where's my boat?"

Shep looked beyond him to the open water behind the fireboat. Nothing.

"Looks like it's gone," he told the distraught sailor.

"Good riddance!" Susie spat. "I say leave it where it is."

Jimmy shook his head, silent.

They were approaching the pier now, and Shep asked if this would be a good spot to put them ashore. A graveled parking lot was located in a small clearing beyond the pier, connected to a nearby highway. A lone pickup was parked next to a No Dumping sign.

"This will be fine," Jimmy said. "That's my truck."

Roddy maneuvered the boat toward the small pier, missed his target by a foot or two, and put the engine in reverse.

"Let me get a little closer," he said, spinning the steering wheel.

A loud splash, and Susie was overboard. The water was only three or four feet deep, and her patience was gone. She thrashed through the water and stormed up the gently sloping bank. Barefooted, she took a few steps on the sharp gravel and let loose more descriptive words regarding who now might well be her *ex*-boyfriend.

With slumped shoulders and a pale, contorted face, Jimmy looked up at Shep.

"Thanks." He looked around at each member of the crew. "All of you."

He clambered over the side and up onto the pier.

"Good luck, Jimmy," Troy said, saluting the shipless captain.

"Time to go," Shep told his engineer. "Let's see what's happening on the big water."

They slowly patrolled the lake, and as the morning drifted into early afternoon, the number of boats multiplied. By three o'clock, hundreds of vessels filled the main channel and the myriad coves. It was party time.

"What do you think about that?" Troy stood beside Shep and pointed to the western sky. Dark, billowing clouds were beginning to appear just over the tree line. The sun was still bright, and the remainder of the horizon was crystal clear.

"Let's take a look." Shep grabbed his smartphone, slid his index finger across its surface, and accessed his weather app. He studied it for a moment and then held it so Troy could take a look. "Just a couple of small clouds is all I see. The weather channel isn't calling for anything major—maybe a 20 percent chance of rain."

"That might be good," Troy responded. "A little rain might send a bunch of these people home."

"Doubt it," Roddy interjected. "Listen. Hear that?"

The thumping of a bass guitar wafted across the water. A moment later the words of "I Love Beach Music" had Troy nodding his head and swaying to the familiar music.

"Must be a party at the Point," Shep remarked. "Let's go check it out."

The engine cranked up a couple of notches, and they headed up the main channel and around a distant bend. As they cleared the tree-lined coast, Mason's Point came into view. The sandbar was jammed with a crowd of young people. A large houseboat was anchored 20 yards off the bank, its lower deck alive with dancing, singing, and—most likely—drinking. On top of the structure was a live band, surrounded by speakers, amplifiers, and partying dancers.

"It's only the middle of the afternoon," Troy lamented. "Wait till it gets dark."

The crew's assignment was to ensure public safety. That meant monitoring for excessive alcohol consumption, as well as being vigilant for boats with drunk drivers and possible accidents and mishaps. More than one person had drowned in this lake on previous holidays.

They could be reached through the 911 dispatcher should someone need help, but so far the radio had been silent.

The fireboat cruised past the Point, its crew surveying the scene for anything unusual. Nothing out of the ordinary—just a bunch of young people having a good time.

They meandered up the lake's eastern shoreline, turned slowly around, and retraced their wake.

"You sure there's nothing on the weather channel?" Troy was pointing at the horizon again. More black clouds were gathering—larger and more threatening than before.

Shep looked at his phone. "Seems to be changing some." He glanced up at the black and threatening cloud bank.

Troy looked over Shep's shoulder at the small screen.

"Hmm…where did that come from?"

In the middle of the radar, just west of Lake McDowell, an ugly red blotch had formed, indicating a rapidly approaching weather cell. As they watched, a scrawl appeared, warning of severe weather with high winds and possible hail.

Shem turned to his engineer. "Roddy, head back to the Point. We need to get those kids out of there. A storm's heading this way, and it looks mean."

The boat's engine roared to life. They would be back to the Point in ten minutes, leaving them plenty of time to warn the people on the sandbar and on the houseboat.

Or so they thought. The storm blew up out of nowhere and seemed focused on Lake McDowell. The wind picked up, sending sprays of water over the boat and crew, and the sky—moments ago clear and bright—was now dark and menacing.

The wind came alive with sudden, violent gusts, and the lake turned into a churning cauldron. The fireboat was pelted with waves two to three feet high, raising it out of the water before sending it crashing down again.

They held on to whatever they could find and ducked their heads into the wind and driving rain. The boat skipped past a wooded outcropping of coastline, turned south, and headed for the Point.

Visibility was reduced to a few dozen yards, and Roddy had to back off on the engine. Up ahead, they heard frantic voices and motors revving. There was no more beach music, and when they caught their next glimpse of the houseboat, it was heading into a nearby cove at full speed. Both decks were crowded, and the band was scurrying to find cover for their instruments and sound equipment.

The sandbar was a churning mass of people grabbing blankets and baskets and whatever they could get into their arms. The waist-deep water between the shore and the bar was crowded with waders struggling to get out of the storm. Shep could see dozens of figures hunkered down under the pine trees, apparently determined to wait this thing out.

A low-pitched growl of thunder rumbled across the lake, followed by a flash of lightning. A couple of screams came from the direction of the pines, and Shep realized their danger. The tall trees could act as lightning rods, putting all of them at risk.

He was about to say something to Roddy when Troy pounded his shoulder.

Shep spun around. Troy was pointing over the bow of the boat and saying something unintelligible.

"What?" Shep yelled at him.

Troy leaned close and cupped his mouth over Shep's ear. "There are 30 or 40 kids out there."

Shep looked again. Troy was right. Fifty yards from the sandbar, toward the middle of the lake, he could see heads bobbing in the water. The waves were still as high as three feet, and the wind was still whipping the surface with gusts that came close to blowing the crew overboard. Whoever these swimmers were, they seemed confused and disoriented—moving in circles, if at all.

"Roddy," Shep yelled at the engineer. "Take us over there." He pointed to the cluster of bodies.

As the boat eased toward the group, Troy let down the boarding ramp. He glanced around the boat, wondering if there was enough room for all these people.

"Help! Over here!"

Some of the swimmers saw them approach and started flailing in the direction of the approaching boat.

"Take it easy!" Shep directed them. "We're going to get you all out of the water."

Within a few minutes, the group was either in the fireboat, scrambling over the boarding ramp, or clinging to the side. They were wet and shivering but safe.

"Good work, guys," Shep told his crew.

Another peal of thunder and a blinding flash of lightning caused everyone on board to cringe and duck.

"Let's get out of here," Shep told Roddy.

Lanny Woods had been passing out the few blankets they had on board and was standing next to Shep. The sky exploded again, and the surface of the lake was bathed in an eerie, gray-green blast of light.

"Look, Shep—over there." Lanny pointed over his captain's shoulder to an area of water 60 or 70 yards distant. Two heads appeared then disappeared between plummeting waves.

Shep surveyed the water around him. The boat was headed in the opposite direction and there were still at least a dozen people who needed to be helped onboard.

"Here." He handed his phone to Lanny, took a couple of strides to the side of the boat, and dove into the churning water.

Lanny watched helplessly as Shep took long, powerful strokes toward the distant couple.

"Over here!"

It was a faint, terrified cry—the voice of a young woman.

"We're over here!"

Shep swam toward the voice and almost ran into her. Early twenties, with her hair wet and matted across her face, she clung desperately to a noodle—an inflatable device that was thus far saving her life.

"Are you okay on this thing?" Shep asked her.

She nodded and then pointed behind her.

"We got separated, and Jesse doesn't have anything to hold on to."

Shep scanned the water and saw something moving. It was a hand, waving weakly above the waves.

"Can you see the boat?" he asked the young woman.

"Yeah. Over there." She pointed behind him.

"Swim toward it and don't stop. Okay?"

"Okay."

She clutched the noodle to her chest and started kicking.

Shep looked back for the waving hand. There it was again, and he started swimming toward it. He was a few yards away when he caught a glimpse of Jesse. The young man's eyes were glazed and his mouth hung open and slack. His arms were barely moving now—a weak and ineffective dog paddle.

"Jesse!" Shep yelled.

The man's eyebrows raised a little, and he seemed to focus on his rescuer. His hand went up in the air again, but then his eyes closed, and he disappeared beneath the surface of the water.

Shep was ten feet away. He took two quick, long strokes and then dove. Blindly, his hands searched beneath him, making ever-larger circles in the murky water. Nothing. He kicked again, going deeper. His right hand brushed against something. He grabbed for it, and whatever it was slipped through his fingers. Another kick and he went deeper. His lungs were bursting—he needed air.

Another bump against the back of his hand. He lunged, grabbed Jesse's forearm, and kicked hard for the surface.

The young man's body was limp. Shep had an arm under Jesse's chest and propelled both of them into the air. He gasped for breath, spewing lake water as he twisted his head, searching for the boat or the Point—something to get him oriented.

He saw lights and began swimming—slow, heavy strokes. It was only then that he remembered he was fully clothed.

Got to get these shoes off. Got to—

"Over there!" Troy was standing at the bow of the fireboat, jabbing his finger in the air, pointing at the two men. "Roddy, he's over there!"

The boat eased forward through the water, carefully coming alongside Shep and his lifeless cargo.

Hands—dozens of them—reached out and pulled the two men aboard.

"Get him on his back!" Troy yelled. "And give us some room!"

Shep was on his hands and knees, coughing and gasping. He watched as his crew positioned Jesse on the boat's deck, cleared his airway, and tilted his chin up into the air.

He wasn't breathing. Troy knelt by his side and placed his hands on Jesse's chest, ready to start CPR.

Troy straightened his elbows, checked the position of his interlocked fingers, and…Jesse started coughing. Water spewed from his mouth, and his arms flailed in the air.

The crowd on the boat gasped and then cheered.

Troy tilted Jesse's head to one side, preventing any more aspiration of lake water.

More coughing and gasping and flailing. Within a few minutes, Jesse was sitting up and looking around.

Still on his hands and knees, lost behind the young people surrounding Jesse, Shep watched silently.

Three weeks later, Shep Stevens and his crew sat in the auditorium of one of the buildings in the City Complex. He had submitted a report of the happenings of that afternoon on Lake McDowell, recommending his crew for a Citation of Merit.

They sat a few rows from the front of the room and watched as their chief and the city manager walked onto the raised platform. The city manager carried a glossy wooden plaque. He surveyed the crowded room, saw Jesse, and motioned for him to join them.

There were a few welcoming comments, and then Chief Pritchard took the microphone.

"Shep Stevens."

Shep stood up, glanced around him at his crew, and motioned with his hands for them to stand.

Roddy, Troy, and Lanny looked up at him. They didn't move.

"Shep, come up here," the chief instructed him.

He looked down again at his crew. They remained seated. Troy smiled and nodded.

Shep, confused now, stepped over them and walked toward the platform. When he stood in front of the chief, his crew rose—along with everyone else in the room—and began a loud and long applause.

"Shep Stevens, today we, and especially your crew, want to acknowledge and honor your actions on Lake McDowell this past Fourth of July."

The city manager leaned into the microphone. "And don't forget Jesse."

Jesse took a few awkward steps, reached out, and shook Shep's hand.

"In appreciation of those actions, we want to present you with this."

He handed the plaque to Shep, and the applause grew, filling the room and humbling a surprised and speechless Shep Stevens.

ROCK HILL FIRE DEPARTMENT
has awarded this
MEDAL OF VALOR
to
Captain Shepherd Stevens

On July 4, 2015, Fireboat 23 was patrolling the Lake McDowell area when a storm moved in, causing lake conditions to suddenly deteriorate. Fireboat 23 moved into position in a popular area of the lake referred to as the Point, ready to take aboard victims who were in the water without floatation devices and were in imminent danger.

Captain Stevens identified a male subject struggling and, without regard for his own safety, swam 50 yards to the area where he had seen the subject descend under the water's surface. He located the subject and brought him up for air. While Captain Stevens and the subject struggled to stay afloat in the rapidly deteriorating and extremely hazardous conditions, Fireboat 23 moved into position to recover them safely.

For these life-saving actions and this demonstration of bravery during the harshest of conditions, Captain Shepherd Stevens is awarded the Rock Hill Fire Department Medal of Valor.

Nate Pritchard, Fire Chief
October 10, 2015

The ordinary man is involved in action; the hero acts.
An enormous difference.
HENRY MILLER

13

Amber Alert

"911—what's your emergency?"

"It's my baby! Daisy! She's gone!"

The woman was screaming, and the dispatcher flinched as she made some notes on the pad in front of her.

"Is she breathing? Does she have a—?"

"No, she's *gone*! Disappeared! Stolen! It's Manny, I know it! He's got her!"

Bradley Weathers and his partner, Jason Bowman, were patrolling the western part of the county when the call came in.

"Missing child. Two years old. Probable Amber Alert: 227 Sandy Springs Road, off Highway 5 just outside Smyrna. Closest unit respond."

"That would be us," Jason said, switching on the vehicle's lights and siren. "Sheriff's Unit 4 responding."

Bradley felt his pulse quicken as he whipped a U-turn in the middle of Hickory Grove Road. He had two small children at home, and dealing with a possible abduction was his biggest fear.

"Hey, slow down, Bradley!" Jason grabbed the dash and glanced at his partner. "We're only five minutes away."

Weathers exhaled loudly and nodded. But he continued to white-knuckle the steering wheel.

He was 28 years old and had been a sheriff's deputy since graduating from the training academy straight out of high school. This was what he had always wanted to do, and he was good at it. But dealing with young children, especially a two-year-old—his daughter Molly's age—was something he dreaded. He knew it was part of the job, but still... Jason was three years younger. He had been a high school football star, known and liked by everyone in the county. His swagger and easygoing, chewing-gum-popping style was an interesting contrast to Bradley's studious, measured approach. They were a good match and worked well together.

"Look—that's it, up ahead on the right." Jason pointed to a graveled road tucked behind a cluster of cedar trees.

Bradley slowed the vehicle and turned onto the drive, the crushed stone crunching beneath the car's tires.

Jason turned off the siren as they eased down the narrow driveway. They passed a few more bushy cedars, and the house came into view. A ramshackle "single wide" with two missing window shutters and a small wooden front porch. The right handrail listed to starboard, inviting disaster should someone actually lean against it.

"Hmm..." Jason scanned the clearing around the mobile home. Red dirt, a few patches of weeds, and a rusting and forsaken tricycle.

The front door burst open, and a young woman bolted down the rickety steps and ran toward the officers. She was barefooted, clad in denim shorts and a sleeveless plaid blouse.

Odd attire, Bradley thought. It was November, two days before Thanksgiving, and there was a chill in the air.

"I know he's got her! I know it!" Delores Grayson took one last, long drag on her cigarette and tossed it into the yard.

Bradley got out of the patrol car, notepad in hand. Jason called the dispatcher and let her know they had arrived. He patted his holstered weapon and stepped out into the waning afternoon daylight.

"I'm Deputy Weathers, and this is—"

"You've got to go get her! I warned him about this, that he better not try it! I want him put in jail!"

"Hold on, ma'am—let's start from the beginning." Bradley opened his notepad and took a ballpoint from his jacket pocket. "Tell me your daughter's name and age, and who you think might have taken her."

Delores shook her head and tried without success to blow an unruly lock of bleached-blonde hair from her forehead.

"Her name is Daisy, Daisy Grayson, and she's two years old. I know where she is, where he took her. You just have to hurry up before he gets scared and takes off."

"Who are we talking about?" Jason walked up beside his partner. "And what makes you think he has your daughter?"

"It's Manny Smithers, her daddy. We split right after Daisy was born, and he's always sneakin' over here to see her. Says that he wants to be a part of her life and that I can't stop him."

Bradley and Jason exchanged a brief glance. Bradley knew Manny Smithers—they all did. Multiple run-ins with the sheriff's department. Nothing really serious and nothing ever violent. Drug violations—mainly marijuana—and a bunch of drunk and disorderly citations. Not exactly an upright citizen, but not a real threat to the community. Yet you never knew.

"He's stayin' at the Sleepy Pines over in York, the run-down motel out on 321. I don't know the room number, but he's got to be there. You guys need to get goin' right now!"

Bradley was writing everything down. He knew the Sleepy Pines. The department responded to calls out there on a weekly basis. And it *was* run-down. No place for any two-year-old.

"Let's back up for just a minute." Bradley looked up from his notes and studied the young woman's face. "When did you first notice Daisy was missing?"

"It was right before I called 911. She was playin' in her bedroom, and I was watchin' TV in the den. I thought I heard a car drive up but didn't pay any attention. The wind does funny things out here, and you hear all kinds of stuff. Then I thought I heard the screen door in the kitchen close. It's just me and Daisy, so I wondered what was goin' on."

"So that's when you went to check on her and found she was gone?" Jason cocked his head and his eyes narrowed.

"No…not right then. I guess I thought…anyway, I called her name, but she didn't answer. She's stubborn sometimes, and that's not unusual. After a couple of minutes, I went to the kitchen to get somethin' to drink and noticed the door was open. The screen part was closed, but it has a spring on it and closes on its own. That's when I knew Manny had slipped in and grabbed her."

"Any chance she's hiding somewhere in the house?" Bradley glanced over her shoulder at the front door. "If she's stubborn, like you say, she might be hiding or—"

"No, I looked everywhere. She ain't in the house or anywhere outside. Manny came and grabbed her. That must have been his truck I heard. It's a beat-up ol' blue Chevy. When you get to the motel, you can't miss it. It ain't got no rear bumper, so maybe you could arrest him for that too."

"Ma'am, we'll need to check the house real quick." Jason took a step toward the mobile home, and Delores jumped in his way.

"I'm tellin' you, she's not here! Manny has her! Don't you hear me?"

Bradley put his hand on his partner's shoulder. They both knew every minute counted with an abduction—even with a likely suspect. They could always come back if they didn't find Daisy with Manny Smithers.

"We'll head over to York and check on Manny," he told her. "Just be sure to stay here and don't go anywhere."

"I'm not budgin' an inch. I want my baby back."

Some clouds had blown in, and as they headed toward York, the late afternoon had the look and feel of early winter. Bradley turned on the heater in the patrol car.

"What ya think, Bradley? If Manny has the girl, do you think he's stupid enough to stay around here? If it were me, I'd be long gone."

Weathers sighed and shook his head. "Manny Smithers may not be the sharpest pencil in the box, but I think you're right. If he has Daisy, he's probably miles away or hiding somewhere."

The Sleepy Pines Motel was 15 minutes from Delores's trailer. Weathers turned into the parking lot and slowly approached what appeared to be the main office.

"Over there—look." Jason pointed to an old blue Chevy pickup, parked in front of unit 10. Its rear bumper was missing.

Bradley eased the patrol car right behind the truck, blocking any attempt at a rapid exit. The two officers quietly got out of the vehicle and didn't close their doors.

Jason cocked his head in the direction of the corner of the single-story, cinder-block building. Unit 10 was at the end, and while most of these motels didn't have any back doors, the officers would need to be sure. They didn't want any sudden surprises—not with a two-year-old girl's safety at risk.

Bradley nodded and drew his service weapon.

Jason silently disappeared around the corner of the building. A moment later, he reappeared and shook his head. Bradley pointed to the door, and the two officers moved in.

They stood there for a moment and listened. Voices…but it was the TV. Bradley looked at his partner and put his hand on the doorknob. Jason silently counted to three with his fingers and Weathers twisted the handle.

It was unlocked, and he pushed it wide open.

The room was dark, but there was just enough light to make out its contents. The TV flickered and blared on a small dressing table to their left, and a double bed had been pushed kitty-corner against the far wall on the right. The figure of a man jumped up and reached under the bed.

Jason was the first into the room, and his nostrils were immediately assaulted by the pungent odor of marijuana. The air hung thick with it, and he held his breath.

"Hold it right there!" Bradley pointed his gun at the man crouched beside the bed. "Stand up and put your hands behind your head."

The shirtless suspect froze, his eyes moving first to Bradley and then back to Jason.

"You heard him," Bowman said, his voice tense. "Stand up now!"

He tossed something under the mattress and jerked upright, his hands reaching for the ceiling.

"It's not mine, I swear!" Manny Smithers blabbered. "I don't know where it came from and I thought I would just smoke…How did you know I was here?"

Smithers was tall and rangy. His dirty blue jeans hung loosely around his slender waist, and Bradley worried they might hit the floor at any moment. His brown hair hung into his eyes, and he sported a spotty and scraggly goatee.

Jason moved quickly to the bathroom. Nothing. And nothing in the small closet. He looked at Bradley and shook his head. Daisy was nowhere to be found.

"Look, if you want to know where I got the weed, I'll tell you. Only don't bust me, okay? I ain't dealin' anymore, and I don't need any more trouble."

"We're looking for your daughter," Jason said, moving toward the door and some fresh air.

"Daisy? What's the matter? What has Delores done now?"

"She called in a missing person, and she thinks you might have gone by the house and grabbed her," Bradley told him. "Any reason for her to think that?"

Manny shook his head and started to drop his arms. A quick motion of Bradley's weapon sent them back toward the ceiling.

"I love that girl, Deputy. And I wouldn't do anything to hurt her. Delores and I don't exactly get along, but I'd never do anything to Daisy. Is that why you're here? Did she tell you I kidnapped my own daughter?"

Bradley glanced at the floor behind the bed and saw the small, "grass"-filled plastic bag. Manny followed his eyes and took a few short steps into the corner of the room.

"Like I said, I'm not dealin' anymore and—"

"You can put your hands down, Manny." Bradley nodded at the bed. "And count yourself lucky. We've got a little girl to find."

He and Jason retraced their route down Hickory Grove Road to Sandy Springs. Delores must have heard the patrol car approach, and she ran into the yard as Bradley cut off the engine.

"Do you have her? Do you have my Daisy? I told you Manny would…"

She was at the side of the vehicle, peering through the windows, searching for her daughter.

"He didn't have her," Jason said. He was walking toward the house and called back over his shoulder. "He said he didn't know anything about it."

"He's lyin'! He must have her hidden somewhere!"

"We'll need to search the house, ma'am, and see if we find any evidence of someone else being here. You haven't noticed anything unusual?"

Delores had on a cotton robe now, and she shivered as she tightly clutched it to her body.

"No, nothin'. I'm tellin' you, he's got her somewhere. It was him and…wait! He has a cousin—Jimmy Wilkes—who lives a couple of miles from here. I bet that's where he took her! You need to go over there and…"

She paused and looked over Bradley's shoulder. A green and well-worn Plymouth Duster drove up the drive and stopped beside the officers' patrol car.

"Grandma!" Delores ran toward the car, bathrobe fluttering in the cold evening air.

Irene Grayson got out of the Duster, slowed by her 80-plus years and crippling arthritis.

"Delores, what's the matter?"

Delores ran into her grandmother's arms and sobbed.

"It's Daisy. Manny came and stole her."

"He what?" Her gaze came to rest on the officer standing behind them. "Bradley Weathers, is that you?"

"Mrs. Grayson, yes, it's me, Bradley."

He was gradually making the connection. He knew Irene Grayson lived somewhere west of York, but many years had passed since she had taught him in Sunday school. Irene and his own grandmother had been good friends, working side by side for more than 40 years in one of the area's textile plants. They had been "doffers," a physically demanding job that required dexterity and rapid hand movements, removing spindles or bobbins from a spinning frame and replacing them with new ones. It took its toll on both women, leaving them with crippled, swollen, and painful hands.

It was a relief to many when automation replaced humans in this task, and then the mills were gone. Irene found work where she could, taught Sunday school at the same small church Bradley and his family attended before they moved to Rock Hill, and buried her husband 15 years earlier when she was 67. She was a rock, a godly woman, and deserving of some peace in her final years. It appeared to Bradley that she spent much of her time tending to her granddaughter Delores and probably finding little peace.

"What's this about Daisy?" Irene continued looking past Delores and straight into Bradley's eyes. "She's been kidnapped?"

"We're not sure, ma'am. Your granddaughter called 911 this afternoon and reported her missing. We've been looking for her and checked out this Manny Smithers guy. He hasn't seen her, or so he says."

Irene shook her head. "He's a confused young man, but I can't imagine he'd ever do anything to hurt that child. He loves her."

"He slipped over here and stole her, Grandma!" Delores exploded. "Who else would have gotten her? Why won't anybody listen to me?"

Delores stepped away from Irene and spun around, facing Bradley.

"Aren't you guys gonna do somethin'? It's almost dark, and I don't know where my daughter is."

"I had no idea this was going on," Irene said quietly. "I live just about a half mile away as the crow flies, and I came over to check on Delores and Daisy and to see if anyone had seen Scamp."

"Scamp?" Jason walked up and looked at Irene. "Who's Scamp?"

"That's her mangy ol' dog," Delores interjected. "Got him from the rescue shelter a couple years ago—part retriever, part shepherd…mostly mutt."

"He's a good dog," Irene spoke calmly. "He never misses his evening meal, and when he didn't come when I whistled, I got worried. He's never done that before, and I'm afraid something's happened to him."

"Humph. More worried about that dog than about Daisy." Delores turned and stomped toward the trailer.

"We haven't seen a dog since we've been here," Bradley said.

"I just thought I'd check," Irene sighed. "But we need to find Daisy. Is there anything I can do?"

"Maybe just try to keep your granddaughter calm." Jason shook his head and glanced in Delores's direction.

"I can at least do that."

Irene took a step toward the house, stopped, and took something out of her coat pocket. It was a long, silver whistle.

"Just thought I'd check." She blew once, and the high-pitched sound pierced the cold, gathering darkness.

Silence.

She blew once more. Again nothing, and she slipped the whistle back into her pocket.

"Did you hear that?" Jason cocked his head. "Blow that thing one more time, ma'am."

Irene retrieved the whistle and blew.

"Hear it? That's a dog somewhere way back behind the trailer." Jason pointed in the direction of the tall pines silhouetted behind the low-lying house.

"That's Scamp." Without another word, she moved with surprising speed in the direction of the faint barking.

There were a few more echoing barks, and the two officers followed Irene to the edge of the woods. The forest was dark, and Bradley and Jason grabbed their flashlights and shone them in the direction of what had become a rumbling, mournful howl.

"He sounds hurt," Irene said. "I've never heard him make that noise before."

They made their way through tangles of briars and thick bushes, getting closer to the source of the howling. If it was Scamp, he wasn't moving.

The underbrush gave way to a small clearing. They stepped into the opening and froze. A large pine had fallen at the edge of this space, and the beams of the officers' flashlights focused on something curled against it.

"Scamp!" Irene took hurried steps toward her dog. "Are you all right…oh my Lord!"

Bradley and Jason were at her side, staring down at the quivering canine. Scamp's tail was thumping against the forest floor, and he blinked into the bright beams of the flashlights.

Curled against him—snuggled, warm, and asleep—was a little girl. "Daisy!" Irene reached down and picked up the sleeping child. "Daisy!"

Scamp got up, shook himself a few times, and pressed his long, lanky body against Irene. He wagged his tail and looked up at the officers. Bradley thought he was smiling.

Sometimes rescuing angels have more than two legs.

This is my advice to you. Love like a dog.

Oliver Tremble

14

The Deep, Dark Woods

Everybody needs beauty as well as bread,
places to play in and pray in
where nature may heal and cheer
and give strength to the body and soul.

JOHN MUIR (1838–1914)

Muir understood the beauty of creation, the importance of communing with nature, and our inextricable and essential link with this wondrous gift from God. Whitey Johnson understood it as well. That's why he chose a life spent out of doors. And it almost killed him.

ER, 8:50 p.m.

"You know who that is, don't you?"

Amy Connors, our unit secretary, tilted her head in the direction of the stretcher rolling down the hallway. It held an elderly man who was being taken back to the Ortho room. He had fallen at the assisted-living facility where he lived, and EMS 1 had called it in as a broken hip.

"No, I didn't see his face." I was standing in front of her on the other side of the counter, writing on the chart of one of our observation patients.

"Whitey Johnson," she informed me. "He was the game warden around here for more than 40 years. Good friends of my daddy. I think they went to high school together, back when Rock Hill High was over on White Street."

"You talking about Whitey?" Denton Roberts stood beside me and dropped his run-report log on the counter. Denton was the lead paramedic on EMS 1 and had just brought in our most recent patient.

"Yeah, I was tellin' Dr. Lesslie who he is," Amy answered. "You think his hip is broken?"

"Looks like it." Denton nodded slowly. "After everything he's been through, just somehow doesn't seem fair. You'd think he'd be entitled to a little peace for a change."

"You're right," Amy agreed. "Wasn't it about a year ago that he broke his shoulder? The good one?"

"Yeah, last summer," Denton answered. "We picked him up then too. He tripped on some loose carpet in his room and fell. Lucky that's all the damage he did."

"*Good* shoulder?" I asked. "What happened to his other one?"

"Sammy Prescott." Amy spit out the words. "That's what happened."

"*Our* Sammy Prescott?" I leaned into the counter and looked down at her.

"Yeah, Sammy, the Friday-night regular. Saves up during the week for some cheap wine or anything that has alcohol in it."

"And then we bring him in," Denton added. "Been going on for years. Heck, he'll probably outlive all of us."

"Wait a minute," I said. "What did Sammy have to do with Whitey Johnson's shoulder?"

"That's a long story, Doc. First you need to know something about Whitey and how he came to be a game warden."

Whitey Johnson finished Rock Hill High School and headed straight for Clemson. There, he got his degree in forestry and was determined to move out west and work in one of the national forests. He had spent most of his early years in the woods—hunting, fishing, camping, or walking just for the sake of it. That's where he found peace—where he was most comfortable. And that's where he wanted to pursue a career.

But the best-laid plans…His father died suddenly, and his mother and younger brothers needed his presence. His aspirations for hours spent in the redwoods would have to be put on hold—as it turned out, on hold forever.

He called one of his Clemson professors for some advice, and was given the idea of contacting the State and inquiring about a possible opening as a game warden. Whitey was a hunter himself and understood game management. He would later learn that *people* management would prove to be the bigger challenge.

Whitey found a job in the upstate, pinned an official badge to his olive-green shirt, and became a game warden. That's how he ran into Amy's father, his high school friend. It was in the middle of a dove field.

"Daddy used to take my brother Johnny and me out every dove season, right around Labor Day. He had some friends who worked hard on a couple of fields, and we always had good hunts."

"You mean they *baited* fields," Denton chuckled. "I've heard some of those tales, and about all the birds they would bring home."

"Wait a minute," I interjected. "When you say *baited*, you mean throwing down some extra wheat seed or something like that?"

"Oh no, nothing as simple as that," Denton began to explain. "What these guys did would get them put in jail if they'd gotten caught. They used wheat seed all right, but they'd dump a bunch into an old barrel then fill it up with brine—really salty water. You let that soak overnight, drain the water, and dry out the seed. Throw a little of that in a field of sunflowers, and once the doves discover it, you can't beat them away with a broom."

"Must be hard to detect," I said.

"You have to taste it, Doc," Denton explained. "That's the only way to know for sure. But after one or two rains, there's no way of knowin', and by then you've probably had all the shootin' you want."

"Well, I never poked around the ground and ate any wheat seeds," Amy confessed. "I just remember that we always had a lot of birds. That's how I learned to shoot a shotgun. Daddy gave me a 4-10 to use—a single-barrel. He always said that if I could hit a dove on the wing with that gun, I could hit one with anything. He used a Remington 12-gauge automatic, and Johnny had an old over-and-under double-barrel. I'd always get my limit, but Johnny couldn't hit the broad side of a barn. Always claimed the barrels were crooked.

"Anyway," she continued, "one day we were out in this field, and there were birds everywhere. I had my earplugs in, and when Johnny walked up and tapped me on my shoulder, I jumped straight up in the air.

"'Look over there,' he said. He was pointing at the tree line, where a man was walking across the field right toward us. Daddy saw him and waved. Turns out it was the new game warden, a guy named Whitey Johnson. He and Daddy were friends, and I sorta relaxed. We had heard of run-ins with the game wardens and some of the trouble they could cause—mainly big fines. But a couple of times some men got sent to jail. Anyway, Whitey walks over and pats Johnny on the head, waves at me, and walks over to Daddy. 'I'll need to check your gun, Bill.'"

"Uh-oh," Denton moaned. "Don't tell me. No plug."

"No plug? What do you mean?" I asked.

Denton shook his head. "If you're in a dove field, you can only shoot three shells at a time. Any more than that is illegal and will get you fined. That's why Whitey didn't mess with Johnny's over-and-under. That gun only holds two shells. And Amy's was a single-barrel—one shell only. But her daddy's automatic would hold up to five shells. That's why you have to put a plug in it—sort of a plastic stick—that limits you to three shells. Go on, Amy. What happened?"

"Well, you're dead right, Denton. Whitey asked Daddy for his gun and ejected all the shells in it. One, two, three. I can see the smile on Daddy's face as plain as day, as if he were standin' right here. Then Whitey started puttin' them back in the gun—one, two, three…He reached into his pocket and took out a couple of shells. Four…five…I thought daddy was gonna fall over when those other shells slid in. Come to find out, there was no plug in the gun, even though Daddy always made sure there was. Well, Whitey handed the shotgun back to him and took a pencil out of his pocket. 'Here, use this as a plug,' he told him. 'But that'll be $200.'"

"Two hundred dollars!" Denton exclaimed. "Right there on the spot?"

"Yep, right there." Amy nodded and smiled. "It was either that or lose his gun and maybe go to jail. Whitey didn't mess around, not even with his friends. He was always fair, but he was gonna do the right thing."

"Why wasn't there a plug in the gun?" I asked her. "If your dad was always careful about that, how did it slip by him?"

"Well, the reason for that cost Johnny a lot of work around the house and yard for a couple of months. He had borrowed Daddy's shotgun to shoot targets in a friend's field—clay pigeons. He took the plug out so he could shoot five shells if he had to, and he forgot to put it back in."

"Sounds like an expensive lesson to me," Denton observed. "And your dad didn't get mad at Whitey?"

"Not for a moment. He respected him and knew he was bein' fair. Actually more than fair. Like I said, he could have confiscated his shotgun or worse. But that was Whitey—he was always fair and always tried to do the right thing."

"All right, but what does that have to do with Sammy Prescott and Whitey's shoulder?" I asked her. "What's the connection there?"

"The connection happened 25 or 30 years ago," Amy began. "I was still in grade school, but I remember Daddy talking about it. In fact, there were a lot of people talking about it, and they were really upset. Sammy was a bad apple, but he wasn't the only one in that family. His father was always in trouble with the law, and Sammy's brother was too."

"Didn't he get shot over in Chester a couple of years ago?" Denton interrupted. "The brother, I mean. Some kind of drug deal?"

"Yeah, shot and killed," Amy said matter-of-factly. "But Sammy was the worst. Everybody knew that, and nobody was surprised when they found out what happened over on old man Bates's property."

"Old man Bates?" I was trying to keep up with her.

"Yeah, you know him, I think. Charlie Bates. Owns a couple hundred acres of land down near the Catawba River. Lots of turkey and deer on the property, and for years Charlie had a hunt club on it. A couple of cabins and everything. Charlie made people toe the line, or they couldn't be members of the club. He ran a tight ship down there, and when he heard some shootin' one day when nobody was supposed to be on the property, he called Whitey Johnson.

"Whitey had only been on the job about a year when it happened. He drove out to Charlie's place, and Charlie told him where he had heard the gunshots. He had taken his Gator through the woods and looked for a poacher but hadn't seen anyone. Hadn't heard any more shooting until he was standin' right there with Whitey. Off in the distance they both heard a couple of rifle shots, and Whitey was on his way. Just took off on foot. Charlie remembers him pullin' his orange vest out of his back pocket and puttin' it on as he disappeared into the woods.

"Whitey had told Charlie to stay put, so he just hung out in the backyard and waited. About a half hour went by, and he heard another shot, maybe two. After a while, a diesel pickup came tearing down the highway right in front of his house. He caught a glimpse of it—a big purple Ford—the kind of truck that Sammy Prescott drove. He couldn't see who was drivin' it—goin' way too fast.

"Charlie didn't put two and two together until he saw a man comin' out of the woods. He was about a hundred yards away and wearin' an orange vest. It was Whitey, and he was walkin' slow and holdin' his shoulder. The whole left side of his shirt was stained dark red. Charlie hollered at him, and when Whitey looked up, he waved and collapsed."

"Sammy Prescott shot him?" I shook my head in disbelief. "It would have been on purpose, with Johnson wearing that vest. You can see those from hundreds of yards away."

"Yes, it was Sammy." Amy was spitting her words again. "And yes, he did it on purpose. Whitey almost bled to death. High-powered round went right through his shoulder. Tore it up real bad. No one could figure out how he made it back to Charlie's house. When the law enforcement division got out there and looked at everything, they said he must have walked almost a mile.

"The way Whitey tells it, after he left Charlie's house, he heard another shot and walked toward where he thought it was coming from. He didn't know Sammy Prescott—not yet. But when he saw him, he hollered out so he'd know he was there, and Sammy turned around, drew down on him, and shot him. Left him to die…or probably thought he had killed him."

"And that was Sammy driving by Charlie's house?" Denton pieced the story together.

"Yeah, that was Sammy," Amy answered. "Trying to get away. Didn't do any good though. By morning he was in jail. And Whitey was in the hospital. That was back in the day before shoulder replacements, and that joint was stiff and painful for a lot of years. Finally had surgery on it a couple of years back and had it replaced. And just so you know what kind of man Whitey Johnson is, he'll tell you that he has Sammy Prescott to thank for his new bionic arm. 'Better than the first one,' he'll say."

"What happened to Prescott?" I asked.

"I think he got ten years for shootin' Whitey," Amy answered. "And then another five for somethin' that happened in prison. Like I said, he's a bad apple. A real bad apple."

"Came right back to Rock Hill," Denton said. "Hasn't shot anybody else, but he manages to stay in trouble. Always into something. He lives by himself now, with his father and brother both dead. Just a mean man with a mean heart."

"That tells you even more about the kind of man Whitey Johnson is," Amy observed. "Just how mean Sammy Prescott is and what Whitey did for him."

Amy sat there for a moment, and my curiosity was about to explode. "What?" I finally asked her. "What did Whitey do for Sammy Prescott?"

"Let me tell him about that one, Amy," Denton said, sliding to the edge of his chair. "I was there and remember it plain as day."

Whitey Johnson was where he wanted to be—in the middle of the woods in a grove of giant white oak trees. They stretched for a couple of miles along Turkey Shoals Creek, a part of the county known for wild turkey and deer. Lots of deer. The acorns from the oaks provided food for a variety of animals and supported the ever-growing deer population. It was also an area frequented by unlicensed deer hunters and those who chose to hunt outside of prescribed hunting seasons—such as this crisp, clear winter morning.

Whitey wasn't responding to a landowner's complaint or any reported disturbance. He was just doing what he loved most about his job—hiking through forests and fields, just observing and "checking on things."

He crossed a small stream and followed it up a ravine to a clearing in the forest. This was one of his favorite spots, and he tried to visit it when he was in these woods. A couple of crows burst into flight from an oak up ahead, and he stopped, startled.

His mind wandered, and he thought of the trivia questions his father used to throw at him. One of those had been the name for a group of these large, loud, black birds.

A murder of crows. Why not a flock, or covey, or something less sinister? Who came up with a murder?

He laughed at himself and then for some reason thought of Sammy Prescott and the ambush years earlier. He rubbed his stiff and painful shoulder, shook his head, and scaled the far side of the ravine.

The clearing was just ahead, and he stopped again, frozen in his tracks. Something wasn't right. His eyes searched every side of the glen. Nothing. Then his gaze climbed into the leafless trees. Strong, muscular branches. Off to his right, a couple of squirrels jumped from limb to limb, spotted the game warden, and scurried out of sight.

A sudden breeze swept hundreds of fallen leaves into small, short-lived eddies. His eyes followed them to the far edge of the clearing. There, partially camouflaged by long-dead branches and brush, was a deer stand. It was rudimentary—a simple ladder made from weather-stained two-by-fours and strapped to a tree. At the top of the ladder, 15 or 20 feet off the ground, some enterprising but ill-advised hunter had lashed an old metal folding chair to the trunk. It was rusting away now, and the whole decrepit structure seemed to dare any thinking person to try to use it.

Whitey looked closer. The top rung of the ladder was snapped in the middle—its fractured ends revealing a lighter, fresher color. It had only recently been broken.

He took a few steps toward the stand and stopped once more, straining his ears. A noise, coming from the base of the tree. Out of habit and painful experience, he knelt on the forest floor and listened.

There it was again, a low, painful moan. Somebody was hurt.

Whitey jumped up and jogged across the clearing. The deer stand was attached to one of the largest oaks in the area—at least five feet in diameter. A boot was visible on the left side of the tree, but the connected body was completely out of sight.

Another moan, and the boot shifted. Whitey hurried toward the tree and stepped around its base. There, sprawled on the ground, was a man dressed in an old camo jacket and tired blue jeans. He was holding his head in his hands with his eyes squeezed shut. Another moan and his right hand reached for his left thigh.

Whitey flinched. The man's left leg was bent at an odd angle, and his left pant leg was torn and stained a dark color. From the middle of his thigh extended a whitish, bloody object—part of his fractured femur.

The game warden's medical training flashed in his brain.

The human body contains about seven units of blood. You can lose at least two units from a fractured femur. And if you don't stop the bleeding, you will die.

Whitey looked around and felt his pockets for anything that could be used as a tourniquet. Nothing. Then he reached for his belt, unfastened the clasp, and whipped it off.

He knelt beside the man. "Okay, I'm here, and I'm going to help you."

The man took his hands from his face and looked up into Whitey's eyes. They stared at each other without speaking.

Sammy Prescott.

Jimmy Belton had to pull hard on his steering wheel to miss the man standing on the edge of Baker's Creek Road. Even then, his Ford pickup came within inches of hitting the slumping, uniformed figure. He stood bent over, his hands clutching his knees. The man was either exhausted or sick or both.

Jimmy braked and glanced into the rearview mirror.

Whitey Johnson!

Belton threw the truck into reverse and backed toward the game warden. He was 20 yards away when he saw the body lying at Whitey's feet.

Heart pounding and face flushed, Jimmy jumped out of his truck and bolted for the two men.

"Whitey, what's goin' on here?"

It had taken only a split second for Whitey to get over the shock of seeing Sammy Prescott lying in front of him. And only another one for him to tie the belt above Sammy's open and fractured femur. He would be able to stop the bleeding, but he wouldn't be able to do anything about the pain.

"Sammy, I've got to get you out of here. You've lost a lot of blood, and we need to get to a hospital. I don't have time to get back to my truck, so I'm going to have to carry you."

Whitey paused. Sammy's eyes were closed.

"Sammy, do you hear me?" Whitey thought he saw a nod of the man's head.

"This is not going to be any fun," the game warden told him. "That leg is going to hurt, but I can't help it."

He squatted beside the man, slid his arms under the limp body, and staggered to a standing position.

Sammy screamed in pain—the first of many that would fill the quiet, peaceful woods.

Whitey adjusted the deadweight in his arms, and his own injured and scarred shoulder silently screamed, joining Sammy's piercing wails.

Denton took a breath and shook his head.

"Doc, when the sheriff's deputies went out there the next day, they figured Whitey had carried him almost three miles. That's rough terrain, with a couple of creeks and gullies. It's tough just walking it, much less carrying any kind of a load. It wore Whitey out, but it saved Sammy's life. Jimmy Belton called 911 from out on Baker's Creek Road, and I was on the unit that responded. Sammy had just about bled to death. Ended up being in the hospital for a couple of months, I think."

"And that's what finally ruined Whitey's shoulder," Amy added. "Or what was left of it. That's what led to his shoulder replacement, and why he jokes that Sammy Prescott was responsible for him getting a new one."

"I'm not sure he's joking," Denton said. "That's just Whitey. He doesn't bear any grudge toward Sammy. If he did, he could have just left him in the woods—like a lot of men might have done. But not Whitey."

I picked up the chart for the Ortho room. "Whitey Johnson—78-year-old male—injured hip. Sounds like this is someone I need to meet."

The first question which the priest and Levite asked was:
"If I stop and help this man, what will happen to me?"
But…the good Samaritan reversed the question:
"If I do not stop and help this man, what will happen to him?"
Martin Luther King Jr.

15

"911—What's Your Emergency?"

ER, Saturday afternoon

Amy, the man in 5 needs a chest X-ray and some blood work. And let Triage know his wife can come back now."

I slid the man's chart across the countertop to the unit secretary and then picked up the record of the next patient to be seen.

The Triage door opened behind me. I heard a familiar voice and turned around. Lori Davidson was pushing a wheelchair occupied by a middle-aged woman into the department. Her right leg was crossed over her left, and she clutched a bloody towel over her injured right foot. I studied her face, trying to place the voice.

"Just somethin' stupid, Doc." She looked up at me and shook her head. "I've told my kids and grandkids never to go in the lake barefooted. Never know what you're gonna step on. Shoulda known better than to wear my Crocs. One of them came off when I was in the water, and when I stepped down—the very next step!—I sliced my foot on a piece of glass. Somebody's busted beer bottle, I guess. I really did a number on it."

Lori's eyes widened, and she nodded. "Pretty good cut. And pretty dirty."

I was still struggling to match the voice with a name—this was somebody I knew.

Amy spoke up and solved the mystery. "Arlene! What have you gone and done now? And why didn't you call in the emergency?"

Amy was kidding, but I immediately recognized the name and made the connection. Arlene Adams was a 911 dispatcher and had been at the job for more than 20 years. We had never met, but I had listened to her voice and talked with her on hundreds of occasions.

"Sorry we get to meet this way, Doc."

Lori wheeled her down the hallway to Minor Trauma and one of our empty stretchers. I took care of the child in room 4, tossed the chart into the discharge rack, and headed to Minor and Arlene Adams.

Arlene was right. She had really done a number on her foot. A deep, curved laceration extended five inches from her instep, across the ball of the foot, and ended between her great and second toes. I couldn't stop my eyebrows from raising. Any laceration between any toes is going to be difficult to repair.

"Gonna take a while, isn't it?" she asked.

"You're right about that, Arlene."

Lori had pulled over a metal stand and was opening a suture kit. After injecting the wound with a local anesthetic, I sat down and went to work.

"Well, I guess this will give us a chance to talk for a while," I said. "Sorta get to know each other." She shifted on the stretcher, making herself comfortable. And we started talking.

"Okay, Arlene, so tell me. What are some of the most unusual 911 calls you've ever gotten? You've been doing this awhile, so I'm sure you've heard it all."

"You can bet on that, Dr. Lesslie. One of the strangest involved you."

"Imagine that," Lori muttered behind me.

"Me?" I looked up at Arlene. "Tell me about it."

"It was around midnight," she began. "A call came in from the Hardee's near the hospital. A woman called in with chest pain and said she needed an ambulance. The place is only a couple hundred yards from the ER, but she sounded like she was upset, so I told her to sit down and wait on EMS. We sent out a unit, and they were there in a matter of minutes."

I leaned back and folded my gloved hands.

"I remember the night you're talking about. Can't place the name, but I can see the woman's face. The ER was crazy, and the waiting room was packed. She had come in earlier with some vague complaint of itching or something, and the triage nurse checked her vital signs and asked her to take a seat. We had some really sick people in the department, and it was going to take a while to get to the minor complaints. She kept getting up and shouting at the secretaries. Said she didn't care if somebody was having a heart attack—she needed to be seen, and right then. Someone finally called security, and she calmed down for a while. Then she just disappeared."

"That's when she left the hospital," Lori interjected. "And walked through the field to the Hardee's."

"And that's when she called me." Arlene shook her head. "Somethin' wasn't quite right, but I had no way of knowin'. Not until one of the paramedics called later and told me what happened in the ER."

"I'll never forget the look on her face," Lori said. "She came through the ambulance entrance doors on that stretcher, and they stopped right beside me. I had seen her acting out in the waiting room and recognized her right away. You knew who she was too, Dr. Lesslie. She was clutching her chest and rolling around. You walked over, checked her pulse, and told me to take her back out to the waiting room. She could wait her turn."

"You missed that part, Arlene," I told her. "She jumped off the stretcher, stuck her fist in my face, colorfully described some of my ancestry, and stormed out of the ER. Never saw her again."

"Well, actually we did," Lori said. "She came back in the next morning and was diagnosed with pinworms."

Arlene laughed. "Can't imagine why she didn't call 911 then. That would have been a *real* emergency."

"Speaking of real emergencies," I said, "I think you were on duty when the eight-year-old boy called 911 about his father—the man who almost severed his left arm with a chain saw."

Arlene's face sobered, and she took a deep breath. "That was me, and I'll never forget it."

"You shouldn't," Lori told her. "You saved that man's life."

"No, the boy did. I just tried to help."

"911—what's your emergency?"

"It's my dad!" The voice was that of a small boy, desperate and choked with tears. "There's blood everywhere! I need help!"

"Try to calm down, son." Arlene spoke quietly into the phone, pen in hand and now sitting on the edge of her chair. "Tell me where you are and what's going on."

"I'm in the field behind our house! And Dad isn't saying anything! I need help! He's dyin'!"

"Okay. Can you tell me your name and where you live?" The boy's phone number was flashing on the computer screen in front of Arlene. It was a cell phone, and she was trying to ID the location and address.

"Ben! My name is Ben and I live...I live on Whitehurst Street."

Arlene had the address and picked up the Dispatch radio. "Any available unit, respond to 217 Whitehurst Street. Unknown emergency. Child on the scene."

She hung up the radio receiver and spoke again to the boy. "Okay, Ben. Tell me what happened."

The boy's father had been taking down a dead pine tree in the field behind the house. When it started to fall, the tree suddenly twisted, jerking the chain saw toward him. The saw struck his left arm halfway between the elbow and shoulder. Ben was standing 20 yards away and watched as his father stared at his dangling arm. His eyes were wide, unbelieving. And then the bleeding started. Bursts of bright red liquid filled the air, and he collapsed.

"Ben, call for help," he whispered to his son. He had the presence of mind to place his right hand over the jagged, gaping wound, trying to staunch the flow of blood. "In my back pocket—hurry."

The boy retrieved the cell phone from his father's pants pocket and dialed 911.

"Ben, EMS is on the way." Arlene's words were calm and soothing, but she was flushed and sweating. "How is your father now?"

"I think he's dyin'!" the boy repeated. His father was unresponsive. His right hand was no longer over the wound, and blood was flowing freely.

"I don't know how to stop the blood!"

The next few moments saved the man's life. Arlene told Ben to take off his shirt, twist it into a makeshift tourniquet, and tie it above the wound.

"How...how tight do I make it?" Ben was out of breath and crying.

"As tight as you can, son. Keep twisting it until the bleeding stops."

Ben did what she asked. When the paramedics arrived a few minutes later, they found the boy kneeling beside his father, gripping the bloody shirt around the man's arm. At first the boy wouldn't let go—he just shook his head and maintained his grip. Finally, they were able to pry his small fingers from the cloth. He crumpled over his father's body, hugging the man's head.

"Ben, are you there?"

Arlene had never hung up and was still on the phone. One of the paramedics heard her and picked it up. "We're on the scene. The man's got a pulse, but just barely. Good work."

"That *was* good work," I told Arlene. "I wasn't here when they brought him in, but I heard about it. The chain saw went through half of his humerus and severed the brachial artery. It was close, but he made it—and kept his arm. He would have bled to death if you hadn't been able to calm the boy down and have him apply that tourniquet."

"It was the boy, not me," she said. "Sometimes it works out. And sometimes it doesn't."

She was silent for a moment, and then she told us of an experience that didn't work out—one that haunts her to this day.

"Okay, ma'am, please calm down."

The 911 call had come in at three a.m. The woman was crying and wouldn't stop talking. None of it made any sense, and Arlene had no idea of the nature of the emergency.

Finally, the woman paused—probably exhausted from her constant rant.

"Now, can you tell me your problem? Do you need an ambulance?"

This time the woman's voice was quiet—her words measured.

"I think he's going to kill me."

Arlene sat back in her chair, stunned.

"Who's going to kill you, ma'am?"

"My husband," was the terse reply.

"Is he there with you now?"

Her husband had left the house moments earlier, but not before savagely punching his wife in her chest and abdomen. He had spared her face—as he always did—to avoid leaving obvious and telltale bruises. At least up to this point. The violence was worsening, as was his drinking. Every night there was an argument, and every night there was a beating.

"I'll call the police," Arlene told her, reaching for the Dispatch radio.

"No! Please don't!"

There was silence on the phone, and Arlene held the radio in midair.

"I don't want them involved. It will only make things worse."

Arlene spent the next 15 minutes trying to convince the woman to leave the house for a shelter and to get the police involved. This was escalating, and Arlene was afraid of where it might end.

For a moment—a brief, flickering instant of hope—the woman seemed to be listening. She almost seemed to be willing to follow Arlene's advice and leave. And then the flicker was gone.

"No, I can't have you call the police. I'm going to try and make this work. I know he loves me, and I'll try to do better. I'll try not to make him angry when he comes home and maybe then he won't…"

Arlene didn't even know her name. "Ma'am, if you will only—"

A click from the other end, and she was gone.

Two days later, Arlene walked into the call center and sat down to start her shift. A sealed envelope with her name on it was waiting by her computer. She picked it up, curious. The handwriting was that of one of her coworkers.

"Just wanted to be sure you knew. The woman you talked with the other night—the one whose husband has been beating her—was found dead this morning by her neighbors. Her husband is in custody and has confessed. I'm sure you did everything you could."

Had she? She had called the police in spite of the woman's objections. When they arrived at the house, she had denied any problems with her husband, any physical abuse. There were no bruises to be seen, and the officers left, powerless to intervene. But had she done enough? Could she have somehow insisted the woman leave and seek protection? And if she had, would she be alive today?

"Arlene, you did everything anyone could do." Lori stroked the woman's arm and looked over at me, shaking her head. "I can't imagine being in that kind of position. It's tough enough here in the ER, but at least we can put our hands on someone—do what we must to help them. When you're on the phone and can't even see them, you must feel—"

"Helpless," Arlene finished her sentence. "You feel helpless. And powerless. When she hung up the phone, I knew something bad was going to happen. And it did."

"But not always," I said, trying to change the somber mood in the room. "I remember a couple of months ago when officer Sudderth brought in that man over off Celanese Road. The guy who threatened to kill himself, remember? Sudderth told me that you somehow talked him down—that you saved the man's life."

Arlene heaved a sigh and managed a smile. "Jimmy Sudderth might be exaggerating a little bit, but I do remember that call. It was a Sunday afternoon, just a couple of days before Christmas. Seems like the holidays are always bad for this kind of stuff. People are lonely and depressed, I guess. And sometimes they get desperate."

Will Masterson was all of that—lonely, depressed, and desperate. He wasn't sure why he called 911, but it turned out to be what saved his life. That and Arlene Adams.

"911—what's your emergency?"

No answer on the other end. Arlene could hear breathing—slow and regular.

"Do you have an emergency?"

She wasn't going to hang up until she got a response. She was about to repeat her question when…

"I'm going to do it."

She cocked her head. "Sir, do what?"

"I'm going to blow my brains out."

The words were strangely calm, matter-of-fact. Almost as if the man had been ordering his dinner.

"Excuse me, could you repeat that?"

"I said I'm going to blow my brains out."

Arlene had never faced this kind of situation. She had been trained for this and thought she was prepared. But when the moment came, she was terrified.

When she spoke, her calm, composed words belied her underlying anxiety.

"May I have your name? I'd like to talk with you about this."

"Joe. Just call me Joe."

She scribbled the name on a pad of paper, shook her head, and marked through it.

"Okay, Joe. What's the problem? How can I help? You *did* call 911, after all."

Mistake! She squinted, frowned, and shook her head. She hadn't meant to, but the words sounded confrontational—something she had to avoid.

"Excuse me?"

"I asked how I could help, Joe. What's the problem?"

"The problem is not the problem." He paused for a second. "Hey, get that? The problem is not the problem. I like that."

"Well, what is the—"

"I said it doesn't matter about the problem. The reality is that I'm going to blow my brains out. I'm done. Finished. And I wanted someone to talk to when it happens."

There was a metallic click—the sound of a gun safety being switched off—and Arlene froze.

"Joe, hold on there."

She scanned the computer screen, trying desperately to find his location and address—knowing that if any help was dispatched, it would be too late. There was no nervousness, no hint of doubt in his voice.

Yet they continued to talk. Joe responded to some of her questions— even expanded on them and offered his thoughts about his life and family. But she was running out of ideas, out of questions. She knew that at any moment there would be the explosion of the gun and it would be over.

"Joe, what do you like to do on a Sunday afternoon?"

Where had that question come from? Why had that popped into her mind?

"What? Sunday afternoon?"

He was silent for a moment. Arlene thought she had finally done it, finally pushed him over the edge. She closed her eyes.

"Sunday afternoon," he repeated, the words drawn out, reflective.

He reminisced about fall afternoons spent with his father watching the Washington Redskins on TV and playing touch football in the backyard. Then there were the laid-back college weekends with little to do and plenty of time to do it in.

She let him talk and found herself relaxing a little. Maybe…just maybe…

Another click, and she braced herself, ready for the blast.

And then the sobs.

"Joe, it's all right. Let me send someone over to help."

Quiet, pained sobbing.

He gave her his address, and within 15 minutes two police officers were knocking at his door. The handgun was lying on the kitchen table when they entered the house—loaded, with a bullet in the chamber.

"Turns out 'Joe' was really Will Masterson," Arlene told us. "You guys had him voluntarily committed, and he really did well. Got things straight and turned his life around. I never found out what caused him to reach his breaking point that night, but we stay in touch. Actually *he* calls *me* sometimes, just to check on how I'm doing and to thank me for that night."

"He *should* thank you, Arlene," Lori said. "You saved his life. But whatever made you ask about Sunday afternoons? Where did that come from?"

"I have no idea," Arlene answered, shaking her head. "At that point, all I could do was pray. 'Lord, tell me what to say. Put your words in my mouth.' I was out of ideas, out of things to say. And then I asked about Sunday afternoons. Surprised me as much as it did him, I think. But that seems to be the way it works, doesn't it? You pray for help and it happens. Some people might think that's crazy, but that's what happened."

"We don't think it's crazy," I said, leaning back and stretching. I was almost finished but had to tackle the remaining laceration between her toes.

"Lori, I'm going to need your help here. If you could put on some gloves and hold those toes apart so I can see, I can get this done."

"Sounds like she's gonna help you deliver a baby," Arlene chuckled. "That reminds me of Marlene Struble and the birth of her first child."

"What?" Lori asked, snapping her exam gloves over outstretched fingers. "Marlene who?"

"She was a young girl—18, I think—who lived over beyond Sharon, way on the other side of the county. She called 911 in the middle of the night and said there was a big wet spot in the middle of her bed. It took a while for her to tell me she was nine months pregnant, but when she finally did, I panicked. Her water broke, and she was a good 30 minutes from the nearest hospital. About the same amount of time for an EMS unit to get there. And then what would *they* do?"

"Well, what did *you* do?" Lori looked up at Arlene, transfixed.

"I did what any good 911 dispatcher would do. I grabbed my manual and turned to the section on delivering a baby."

"Wait a minute." I sat up straight and stared at her. "Is there really such a thing? A delivery manual for 911 operators?"

"Well, not exactly," Arlene confessed. "But I kept a childbirth manual at my desk just in case. One of my instructors had recommended it, but she said not to even consider using it unless I was faced with a dire emergency. I figured this was dire enough, so I pulled it out."

"So what happened?" Lori asked.

"Well, first I dispatched an EMS unit and told them what to expect. Then I turned to the first page. Actually, by this time she was already on page 20, so I knew we needed to get started."

"Okay, back up a minute," I interrupted. "This was her first baby, right?"

"That's right. First one."

"Did you think you might have some time to get her to the hospital before she delivered? First babies can take a while."

"Oh really, Dr. Lesslie?" She cocked her head at me. "How many babies have you had? And just where were you when I had my fourth child?"

She had whipped me. "Okay, go on."

"Like I said, she was a good 30 minutes from any help, and I needed to do something. There was nobody at home with her, and she had no way to drive anywhere. That, plus the fact that she was crownin'."

"What?" Lori's eyes widened and her jaw dropped. "You didn't tell us that part."

"Must have forgotten. Or you guys kept interrupting. But yes, she told me what was happening, and from her description, I could tell she was crownin'. Didn't take long after that—about 20 minutes—and she had her son in her arms. That was the first time I've been happy to hear someone screaming in the background over the phone, I can tell you.

But everybody did fine. EMS got there just in time to clamp and cut the cord—told them how to do that too. They got her and the baby to the hospital, and they were both home in a couple of days."

"What a great story," I told her. "A long-distance delivery, and it worked."

"It did, and boy was I relieved. And if you ever need a delivery manual, Doc, I keep mine right beside me every shift I work."

And with that, I tied off her last suture, stood up, and stretched my aching back.

Arlene sat up and examined my handiwork.

"Not too bad, Doc. Thanks."

"Glad to help, Arlene. And thanks for the stories. I know there are a lot of people out there who are glad you're on the other end of 911."

"Well, I don't know about that. But there was one lady who was pretty happy. She had a major emergency, and I was able to help."

I had stripped off my gloves and was heading out the door—but I knew this might be good, so I stopped and turned around.

"Yeah? Tell us about it."

Lori was dressing Arlene's foot. She paused and looked down at the woman.

"Well, it was a couple of years back—right around Thanksgiving. See? Holidays again! Anyway, my line rang and I picked it up."

"911—what's your emergency?"

"I'm in a world of trouble." A woman's voice—strained and tearful.

"How can we help?" Arlene held a pen over her pad of paper and waited.

"I'm at my wit's end and don't know where to turn."

The woman was growing more desperate, and Arlene persisted. "Ma'am, I need to know the nature of your emergency. How can I help you?"

A long pause, and Arlene grew anxious.

"Honey," the woman began, "I've got about 18 family members coming to the house for Thanksgiving, and they all expect me to have turkey. I have no idea how to cook one. I've never been able to get it right—too dry, too done. I need help, and I was wondering if you might give me some advice. Everybody always says to call 911 when you need help."

"What?" Lori was shocked. "You've got to be kidding! She called 911 to find out how to cook a turkey?"

"She was desperate," Arlene said flatly with a twinkle in her eye.

"Let me guess," I said, heading toward the doorway. "You just happened to have a recipe in the back of your childbirth manual."

"Well, as a matter of fact…"

> *The purpose of life is not to be happy.*
> *It is to be useful,*
> *to be honorable, to be compassionate,*
> *to have it make some difference that you have lived*
> *and lived well.*
>
> RALPH WALDO EMERSON

16

Three...Four...Five

July 4, 6:48 p.m.

Ricky Spruill and Randy McIntosh were playing Hearts at the western headquarters of the York County Rescue Squad when the call came in. It was sheer coincidence that they were still there, having just restocked their ambulance after responding to a timber truck that had rolled over. Some might call it pure luck. Whether it was good luck or bad luck...well, that determination would be made over the next few hours.

"You guys ready for another call?"

It was the EMS dispatcher, and Ricky thought she sounded nervous. He pushed the speakerphone button, and Randy leaned across the table.

"What ya got?"

"Gunshots fired near Bullock's Creek—114 Cedar Creek Road. Reports of one person wounded, maybe a couple. We have EMS 2 en route, but you're closer and I wanted to give you a call."

Randy glanced at his loaded hand of cards, shook his head, and tossed it to the tabletop. Both men were up and headed toward the door.

"We got it," Ricky tossed over his shoulder. He dropped the receiver into its cradle, grabbed his medical bag, and closed the door behind them.

The dispatcher kept talking, unaware they were gone.

"You two be careful. The shooter is allegedly high on something and completely out of control."

Ricky and Randy were members of a dying breed. In the not-too-distant past, local rescue squads were the only responders to auto accidents, heart attacks, and all manner of disasters and calamities. With the advent of EMS systems, these volunteer squads have largely been marginalized in most metropolitan and urban areas, and their days appear to be numbered. But on this hot, steamy summer evening, these two men were once again responding to an emergency in a remote part of the county, and they would be putting their lives on the line.

"Why you goin' this way?" Randy was buckled into the passenger seat and looked at his partner as they hurtled down the left branch of a Y intersection. "Cedar Creek Road is back that way." He thumbed over his right shoulder, brow furrowed.

"You just relax," Ricky chided. "They started some work on Slatter's Bridge last week, and you can't get through. Have to go around and circle back on Adam's Branch Road. A little longer, unless you make the mistake of going all the way to the bridge. Then it's a lot longer."

Randy settled back in his seat and flipped on the unit's siren. "Didn't know that. Glad you did though."

Rows of pine trees melted behind them as they sped down a straight stretch of highway.

"Wonder what's goin' on," Ricky mused. "Haven't had a shooting this side of the county since…I don't know when. Probably someone hunting or somethin' like that. I don't recognize that address on Cedar Creek, and I'm not sure who lives over there. Not many houses, as I recall."

"I think the Benfields live over that way. Ray and his daughter Katlyn. I went to high school with her. Mother died a while ago, and I'm pretty sure she's living with her father. I remember he took it pretty hard."

The road took a sharp right, and Ricky slowed the ambulance, but not before Randy shifted in his seat and slid into the door. He reached out and braced himself against the dash.

"Sorry about that," Ricky chuckled. "Now that you mention it, wasn't Katlyn seeing Rooster McManus? And didn't they have a child a couple of years back?"

"Yep, you're right. How many times have we carried Rooster to the ER after some drunken brawl he's been involved in? Or that time six months ago when we took Katlyn to the ER."

Ricky and Randy had responded to a domestic violence call at a home in York. It was Katlyn's aunt's house, and the young woman was hiding there, having been beaten by Rooster for not having his dinner ready when he got home from deer hunting. She lost two teeth that night and had suffered a fractured cheekbone. Rooster spent three days in jail and was released.

"Katlyn was a smart girl—pretty too," Randy continued. "And I always wondered why she would get hooked up with a guy like him. I guess it's like they say—opposites attract."

"Like you and me," Ricky drawled. "I'm smart and good lookin', and you're—"

"Whoa! Look out!"

A doe and her two fawns darted across the highway, barely yards in front of the speeding ambulance. Ricky swerved, just missing them.

"You want me to drive?" Randy looked at his partner.

"Almost there. Let's see...114—isn't that the address Dispatch gave us?"

He slowed the vehicle, and the two men stared at a weathered mailbox on the right-hand side of the road. It had seen better days, but the numbers were still visible.

"Yep, that's it," Randy answered. "I'll call and let Dispatch know we're here. And we need to know if the sheriff's deputy is here yet. Still don't know what we're getting into."

The ambulance turned onto the rutted, graveled drive, and Ricky slowed to a crawl, dodging a dead and leaning pine tree. He had barely enough room to negotiate the small clearance.

"You'd think Ray Benfield would keep better care of his place," Randy observed.

"I think he's had a tough couple of years, especially with Katlyn and the baby. And before that, his wife."

The driveway wound through a thick, honeysuckled forest of pines and cedar trees, and then it straightened as they approached a small, grassed opening. At the far side of the clearing sat a double-wide—beginning to show its age but surprisingly well kept. The window shutters and trim had recently been painted a deep blue, contrasting with the clean, pale-gray siding. On the wooden front deck, a small tricycle lay on its side just to the right of the open screen door. The door flapped against the side of the trailer, making an eerie thumping that echoed off the tall pines.

Ricky steered the ambulance down the graveled drive and crunched to a stop 30 yards from the house.

"Over there." Randy pointed to the left corner of the structure. A man sat in the sparse grass, leaning against the cinder-block foundation. His head slumped on his chest, and he was clutching his slender belly. Blood seeped through his fingers. He looked up at them with glassy, listless eyes. One arm slowly rose from his abdomen, and a trembling index finger pointed to the front door. He punched the air a few times, mouthed some unheard words, and his arm collapsed again to his lap.

"That's Ray Benfield," Randy said. The two men jerked open their doors and jumped quickly to the ground. "Looks like he's gut shot. I'll get the medical kit."

He glanced around the clearing "I don't see a sheriff's—"

Loud explosions came from within the double-wide, and they froze. Gunshots.

The screen door thumped against the side of the house again—this time much louder. It began to drift closed but was jerked open by a shirtless young man suddenly appearing in the doorway. He was barefoot, and his blue jeans hung low on his narrow hips. Splotches of something red dotted his entire right leg.

"Rooster," Randy whispered.

"He's got to be on something," Ricky said. "Look at those eyes."

Rooster McManus stood with one hand on the frame of the front door, unsteady and needing to prop himself up. His greasy black hair hung haphazardly over his forehead, almost covering his eyes but not quite enough to hide the wide-eyed, crazed-animal glare at Ricky and Randy. He struggled to focus on the two men, shaking his head and blinking fiercely.

"Don't move, Ricky," Randy whispered to his partner. He nodded at Rooster, staring at his left hand. The young man held a .45 revolver, its barrel circling aimlessly, pointed at the porch floor.

Rooster's eyes came to rest on the men and then on the ambulance. The siren was still blaring, and Rooster raised his right hand and rubbed his ear, flinching at the sound. He spread his feet, lifted the revolver, and pointed it in the direction of Ricky and Randy.

"Duck!" Randy yelled.

A shot rang out, and the two men dropped to the gravel. Another shot, and the windshield of the ambulance exploded into a thousand pieces.

Randy looked at Ricky with wide eyes. "What now?"

"Listen," Ricky whispered. "Hear that?"

Randy strained, and in the distance they heard two, maybe three sirens.

"That's EMS and a couple of patrol cars," Randy tried to whisper, but he was too excited—or relieved—and the words croaked incoherently in the driveway. He glanced in the direction of the house and pressed his face against the sharp and unforgiving gravel.

"There's a problem," Ricky said. He nodded in the direction of the sirens. The sound was coming from behind the double-wide, 180 degrees from the way they had approached. "They don't know about the bridge and are coming the wrong way."

"What?" This time fear produced a raspy murmur, and Randy's face paled.

"Once they figure it out, it'll take them another 20 or 30 minutes to get here."

Ray Benfield uttered a pained moan and tightened the grip on his wounded belly.

"Shut up, old man!" Rooster hollered. He pointed his gun at Ray, paused, and changed his target to the two men. Randy burrowed into the gravel.

Rooster stood on the porch and stared at the two men. A devilish grin spread across his contorted face, and he cocked his head toward the doorway.

"Get out here!"

Rooster turned in the doorway, reached behind him, and grabbed Katlyn Benfield by the hair. Her eyes were bloodshot and her face bruised. With surprising strength, Rooster jerked the young woman through the door and tossed her into the yard. She landed on her face— a dull thud followed by all the air in her body escaping through her bloodied and swollen lips.

"You stay put and don't move!" he screamed at her.

He took an unsteady step forward and stared at the ambulance again, wincing at the wailing siren.

"Shut that thing off!"

A whimper, and a small boy appeared in the open door of the trailer. Three, maybe four years old, and wearing only soiled Superman underwear. He clutched a Carolina Panther doll to his chest and sucked on his thumb—lips trembling. The boy's eyes darted from his mother to his grandfather and then to the two EMTs lying in the driveway.

The thumb came out of his mouth. "Mama."

"Shut up, boy!" Rooster spun around and raised a hand, leaning toward the helpless child. "I told you to shut up and stop your snivelin'."

"That's it," Ricky muttered, slowly picking himself up and brushing the dust from his shirt and pants.

"What are you doing?" Randy glanced at his partner and then at Rooster. "Get back down!"

"Ray Benfield is going to bleed to death if he doesn't get help, and Katlyn needs protectin'. And that boy…"

He was on his feet and walking toward Rooster McManus.

"Ricky…" Randy reached out and grabbed his partner's leg, but he shook his hand away and kept walking.

Rooster was standing on the deck and staring up into the afternoon sky, his eyes closed.

It was impossible for Ricky to walk quietly across the gravel, and the sound of his footsteps traveled to Rooster's ears. His head slowly lowered and his eyes opened, coming to rest on the approaching EMT.

Rooster raised the .45 and pointed it at Ricky's face.

"That's about enough, man. Don't come any closer. I done shot the old man—it ain't nothin' for me to shoot you."

Ricky stopped, looking at the slumping Ray Benfield and then at the little boy in the doorway.

"Time for this to end, Rooster. Put down that gun and let us help Mr. Benfield." He started walking again, right into the shiny barrel of the revolver.

"I told you to stop!" Rooster took a step back but didn't lower his gun. "And that old man can bleed to death for all I care. Fillin' Katlyn's head with lies and such. He needs to bleed to death."

The child behind him dropped the doll and bolted down the steps toward his fallen mother.

This was the moment Ricky needed.

In three giant strides, he was up the steps and reaching with both hands toward Rooster.

Rooster had watched with wide eyes as the boy ran down the steps, his gun hand momentarily drifting to his left. But he saw Ricky, raised his arm, and leveled the weapon in his face.

Ricky never flinched.

Rooster pulled the trigger, and the hammer of the weapon fell.

Randy was on his feet and only steps behind his partner. Too late.

He saw the trigger finger curl and tighten and waited for the life-ending explosion. But nothing. Only a metallic click, followed by another, and another.

In a split second Ricky was on top of Rooster. He outweighed the young man by more than a hundred pounds and quickly had him flat on his back. He grabbed the gun and tossed it into the yard.

As spaced-out as Rooster must have been, he knew it was over, and his body crumpled—limp and defeated.

"Go check on Ray," Ricky told his partner. "I hope it's not too late."

Thirty minutes later, the small clearing had erupted into a scene of flashing lights, scurrying uniformed men, and chaos. EMS had arrived and immediately started treating Ray Benfield. He had two IVs going and was given something for pain.

"He's got a good blood pressure and good pulses in his legs," one of the paramedics told Ricky. "Looks like the bullet missed his aorta, but it must have been close. He's lost a lot of blood."

Ray's color was better, and when he saw Ricky looking at him, he nodded.

Rooster McManus was in the back of one of the patrol cars, hands cuffed behind him, head back and screaming something unintelligible. A deputy sheriff closed the back door, muting his unnerving racket.

Katlyn Benfield sat on the steps of the deck, clasping her young boy to her chest. Her eyes were closed, and she rocked from side to side.

"Good work, guys." The county sheriff had responded to the call after hearing of possible gunshots. He wanted to be sure the rescue responders were safe. This kind of thing didn't happen very often. "Looks like it was a difficult situation."

Randy cut his eyes at his partner and remained silent.

"It worked out," Ricky said as he packed loose equipment into their medical kit. "I hope Ray Benfield does okay."

"Thanks to you two, it looks like he will. Again, good work." He turned and walked away.

The two partners stood in silence for a moment, watching the scene grow calm as one vehicle after another began to disappear into the pine trees.

"Ricky, I've got to say—you scared me to death. What possessed you to rush that guy? He had a .45 pointed right at your head."

Ricky took a deep breath and looked up into the darkening sky.

"I knew that if we didn't stop him, somebody else was going to get shot—or worse. And I had been counting."

"Counting? Counting what?"

Ricky looked at his partner. "That revolver holds six bullets—no more. When we got here, I heard two shots fired in the house, remember?"

Randy nodded his head. "But what about the other four?"

"Ray Benfield had at least one in his belly. And Rooster fired one at us and one at the ambulance."

Randy thought for a moment and shook his head. "That's five. What about the other one?"

Ricky was silent, and when he finally spoke, his voice was cracking.

"I didn't know about that one. Three, four, five…I wasn't sure about six. But I knew I had to do something. I couldn't just lie there and wait for something terrible to happen. I asked the Lord to take care of my family, and I jumped up and did what I had to do."

Randy stared at his partner, marveling at the man's commitment and bravery. He put a hand on Ricky's shoulder, and the two stood in the grassy clearing, silent.

Six hours later, Ray Benfield was out of surgery and in the recovery room. He was going to make it. Katlyn and her son had been treated and released from the ER and were on their way to her aunt's house in York.

Rooster McManus was in jail, and six months later would be tried and sentenced to a life behind bars.

At a little after midnight, Ricky locked his front door behind him and walked quietly through the living room and into the bedroom. His wife stirred and sat up.

"Tough day, honey?"

Ricky walked over and sat heavily on the bed. He put his arms around her and held her close.

"Could have been worse."

Courage is being scared to death,
but saddling up anyway.

JOHN WAYNE

17

Let Me Take a Listen

W e need some more help in here!"
Deputy Sheriff Danny Bridges, his partner, and I were struggling to restrain a 22-year-old wild man. The two deputies had picked
him up after being called to a public disturbance at a local fast-food restaurant. They had barely been able to get him to the ER and into Major
Trauma, where we were trying to keep him flat on the stretcher without
him flailing around and hurting someone or falling and hurting himself. So far, we were losing.

He was totally incoherent but strong as an ox—the result of a mix-
ture of PCP, alcohol, and who knows what else. As Danny straddled
the man's chest, his partner tried to keep his legs under control, and I
held his arms above his head, paying close attention to the location of
his mouth and teeth.

"Come on! Is anybody out there?" I yelled again.

Two orderlies and a security guard appeared in the doorway. Still
might not be enough.

Danny was sweating and had all of his weight over the guy's torso.
The officer's top two shirt buttons were gone, victims of this evening's
wrestling match. I saw the surgical scar that started at the top of his sternum and disappeared downward, underneath his shirt.

Odd. Danny couldn't be older than 30, and he had always seemed
to be in good health. He wasn't a smoker and didn't appear to be a likely
candidate for a bypass procedure. And the scar was too fresh to have
been the result of some childhood cardiac repair.

Later, once the effects of the PCP had begun to subside and our young visitor had calmed, Danny and I were sitting behind the nurses' station, exhausted. I remembered the scar and asked him about it.

"Oh, that." He looked at his exposed upper chest and lightly ran a couple of fingers over the raised, reddish healed incision. "Doc, that's a long story."

I glanced over at the patient ID board. There were only a few people in the department and they had all been seen, so I leaned back in my chair. "I've got the time, Danny. Tell me about it."

Danny had grown up in York and had attended the local high school, where he lettered in three different sports. He was a good basketball and football player, but his greatest achievements came in track and field.

"I thought I wanted to be a pole-vaulter," he told me. "I don't know if you've ever tried that, but it's not easy. In fact, it's downright dangerous." His index finger traced a thin, pale scar that was barely visible beneath his chin. "Thought I'd quit while I was ahead—or while I still had one."

He found his niche running the 800 meters and the mile. And he was good. He still holds his high school's record in the mile, and he was a shoo-in to win the state championship his senior season. No one had been able to stay with him all year long, and he was in peak condition when the team headed to Columbia.

"I was ready, Doc. Finely tuned, if I do say so myself. It was early May and warm—almost hot. I remember that, and I remember thinking that's what caused the problem. I was on the fourth lap of the race, coming down the backstretch with a 20-yard lead when it happened. I got light-headed and disoriented. The next thing I knew, I was lying on the infield with my coach fanning me with a towel. I guess I blacked out or something like that. Never happened before, and when I went to see our family doctor, he couldn't explain it. Heart and lungs were fine, and by then my brain was working fine. But that was it for my track career and my chances to win a state championship. Still regret that."

That was the first time Danny had experienced any medical problem. And after a while, it was written off as some kind of a fluke and quickly forgotten.

He wanted to pursue a career in law enforcement, and since one of his cousins was a sheriff's deputy with the county, he thought this would be a good place to start.

"The people at the county sent me to one of the local GPs for a pre-employment exam. When I started filling out the paperwork, I got to the part asking if I had ever blacked out or lost consciousness. I remembered that track meet but decided not to mention it on the form. I didn't think it was important, and I didn't want to mess up my chances of joining the department. I'm not even sure he listened to my chest, but he cleared me, signed the form, and wished me good luck. The next day I had my uniform, badge, and a new title—deputy sheriff. My cousin taught me the ropes, and I fit right in. I think mainly because it was something I had always wanted to do, and I respected the guys and gals in the department."

He leaned back in his chair, and its front two legs raised off the floor. Danny folded his hands behind his head and took a deep breath.

"Training went fine, and pretty soon I had my own patrol car. I was usually assigned to the western side of the county, which as you know is mainly woods and farmland. That was a pretty quiet 12 hours—sometimes too quiet. Heck, I was looking for some action—a little excitement.

"About the most exciting thing I had happen was an old pickup running off the road one night and into a ditch. The driver had been partying a little too much and had no idea what might have caused him to go nose-first into a pretty deep culvert. Another deputy drove up, and he had the bright idea of pushing the truck out of the ditch and back onto the road. Didn't want to call a wrecker since only the front end was in the ditch and it was three in the morning. He was a big ol' boy and determined to give it a try, so I got in the ditch beside him and we started pushing. I was straining for all I was worth, and we had that truck almost out of the ditch when it happened.

"I guess I was straining too hard 'cause all of a sudden my head started spinning and my knees buckled. Didn't pass out, but came pretty darn close. The other deputy didn't notice and just tossed the truck the rest of the way onto the shoulder of the road. It was dark, and I just leaned against the bank for a couple of minutes and collected myself. Pretty soon I was fine and climbed out of the ditch. Felt a little tired, but we had just moved a pickup truck and I *should* have been, right? Well, I took the driver back to the station, finished my shift, and forgot about it."

A couple of red flags had been raised in my brain. "You didn't get checked out after that? After you almost passed out?"

"Checked out? No, I was fine. And besides, I didn't want to draw any attention to myself. The chief was really strict about us being fit for duty, and I wasn't about to risk being taken out of commission. I felt fine and just let it slide. Again."

Danny leaned forward, and his chair came to rest on the floor. He propped his elbows on his knees and shook his head.

"I guess I was mighty stupid…and mighty lucky. If it hadn't a' been for Doc Meadows, I wouldn't be here now."

Larry Meadows was not really a doctor. He had earned this title after serving in the military as a medic, including two tours of active duty overseas. He had seen a lot and knew his stuff. Right after his discharge from the Army, he joined the sheriff's department and had been there since—in spite of the repeated efforts of several of us in the ER to convince him to consider a career in nursing or as a paramedic. He was happy as a deputy sheriff.

But he couldn't get his medic training and expertise out of his blood. If he arrived at the scene of an automobile crash before EMS, he would grab his medic bag and jump in. He had saved more than a few lives doing this—staunching the flow of severed arteries or immobilizing a fractured neck before a sudden movement caused permanent paralysis or worse. Yet he knew his role, and when the paramedics arrived on the scene, he quickly assumed the job of deputy sheriff, securing the site and clearing the area of curious onlookers.

It was only in the sheriff's office that he blurred the margins of his job.

"You know, Dr. Lesslie," Danny continued, "if you sat in your chair for more than a couple of minutes, Doc would be right there at your side, checking your pulse or blood pressure. Some of the guys pretended it bothered them, but they never stopped him. In fact, he picked up several cases of high blood pressure and diagnosed the chief with diabetes. What is it? Polyuria, polydipsia, polyphagia? Going to the bathroom too much, drinking water all the time, and eating whenever you could? Well, he nailed it with the chief and insisted he get medical attention right then. Chief Williams swears to this day that Doc Meadows saved his life."

Danny looked down at his chest and once more traced his surgical scar. "He saved mine too. It was one of those times in the office, right after roll call. We had just been given our assignments, and I was about to get up when Doc walked over. 'You look a little flushed,' he told me. 'Sit back down and let me check your blood pressure.' He already had his medic bag open, so I knew there was no use protesting. I actually did feel a little flushed and let him check my pressure.

"It was 160 over 100. That made me flush even more. My BP had never been that high, and I told him so. 'Sit back and unbutton your shirt,' he said. And then he took his stethoscope and started listening to my heart. He listened a long time, and finally I thought he was just trying to spook me. I was about to get up when he asked, 'How long have you had that murmur?'"

Danny paused and looked straight at me. "Dr. Lesslie, I'd never been told I had a murmur—never in my life. Now I was really flushing—and scared. The next thing I knew, I was in a cardiologist's office in my underwear and a skimpy gown. I'll never forget Dr. Clinkscales listening to my heart—longer than Doc had. He stepped back and shook his head. He hadn't heard anything, and he must have thought that Meadows and I were both crazy and wasting his time.

"'Let me listen once more, just to be sure,' he said. This time he heard something, and I remember him cocking his head and leaning closer.

When he finally stood up, he said we were going to get an echocardio-gram and take a look at my heart valves and everything. I could tell he was worried, and that got me worried too."

Danny blew out a long sigh.

"About an hour later, I was calling my wife and telling her we were going to Charlotte to the hospital and having surgery. Just like that. Right out of the clear blue. The EKG showed that I had something the doctor called HCM—hyper…hyper…"

"Hypertrophic cardiomyopathy," I said. It all made sense. Young, healthy, vague symptoms—if there were any symptoms at all. HCM is the leading cause of sudden death in young athletes and frequently gives no warning signs until you drop dead. That's what makes it so scary.

"Yeah, that's right. This HCM is sneaky stuff, and the way the cardi-ologist explained it, those funny episodes I had in the past were probably all related to it. He said that straining—like the time I helped push the truck out of the ditch—can cause light-headedness or a blackout…or worse. I still don't understand how part of your heart can get bigger and cause problems, but I guess it does. After the EKG, I had a heart cath, and everybody that looked at me agreed surgery would be the best treat-ment. I think I had reached a critical point, and the next time doing some kind of unusual exercise or heavy straining might have been the end of things."

The ambulance entrance doors opened and the paramedics of EMS 2 rolled their stretcher into the department. A wide-eyed, five-year-old boy lay clutching his right forearm—the victim of a trampoline mishap.

Danny stood and stretched. "Looks like you've got work to do. And I need to get back on the road." He rolled his chair under the counter, smiled, and pointed to his chest. "Anyway, that's the story with this scar. Doc Meadows saved my life. He's a little peculiar and very type A, but if it wasn't for him, I wouldn't be here. I know that for sure. I'm glad he insisted on taking a listen to me that morning."

The deputy sheriff disappeared through the ambulance entrance and into the night.

I watched as the automatic doors closed and thought about what Danny had just told me. That had been too close. I wondered how many of us have something just as bad, something just as deadly…lurking, waiting. I was thankful for Doc Meadows and for his tenacity.

One person with passion
is better than forty people
merely interested.

E.M. FORSTER

18

Getting It Right

"You know, Doc—we've both been around long enough to see a lot of things change, haven't we?"

Captain Shep Stevens of the Rock Hill Fire Department stood beside me at the nurses' station. He had brought one of his crew members to the ER with second-degree burns on both hands. Their engine company had responded to a brush fire that threatened several homes in a lakeside housing development. The fire was out and the homes had been saved, but his engineer had lost several layers of skin on the backs of his hands. Painful, but he would fully recover.

"You mean how hospital food used to be fairly decent?" I responded.

"Wait a minute—I have a cousin who works in the kitchen here, and the food has gotten pretty good. Or at least I think so."

"Take it easy," I calmed him. "I was just kidding. The food here *is* pretty good. What kind of changes are you talking about?"

"Well," he began, "last week we responded to a 10-50 out on the interstate, and it got me to thinking. Back in the day, when the fire department was dispatched to a motor vehicular accident, we were almost never the first to arrive at the scene. There would usually be some people from a volunteer rescue squad working the accident. A lot of those guys and gals were well trained and did good work. Now though, with all the pressure from local EMS outfits and the hospitals, you almost never see any of those squads. I had a couple of friends who volunteered, and they were always complaining about the lack of money and donations—hard to get equipment and keep stuff up-to-date. A disappearing breed, I suppose. But they helped save a lot of people."

"And now EMS is the first on the scene," I said matter-of-factly.

"Nope, that would be us—the fire department."

I stopped writing on the chart in front of me and turned to him. "I know you guys are first responders, but I would think EMS would get to the scene before you. That's not what happens?"

"Well, 99 percent of the time it's not," Shep explained. "Maybe that happens because of where we're located around the city and county. May not be true everywhere around the country, but it is around here."

"Does that ever cause any problems? Deciding who's in charge or something like that?"

"Not usually. We're always glad to have help, especially with a bad injury or cardiac arrest. I'm sure the paramedics are glad to have some extra hands too. But that's another thing that's changed over the years. More regulations and directives, and it's getting harder to do what needs to be done. Or at least that's the way it seems to me."

This I could understand. In the ER, it was getting more difficult to do the things you knew needed to be done—the things you knew worked. Some might call it the art of medicine, while others would question the medical-legal risk or even the issue of being politically correct. It's hard to always keep those things in mind when somebody's life hangs in the balance.

"Don't get me wrong," Shep went on. "There have been a lot of *good* changes through the years—changes that happened because someone was willing to ask some questions. CPR, for example. That has really changed, just over the past couple of years. That was always a problem when we arrived at the scene of a cardiac arrest. There would usually be a bunch of people standing around—even family members—and no one was doing anything. No chest compressions. No mouth-to-mouth. I can understand the mouth-to-mouth part, especially if it was a total stranger lying on the street in front of you. But everybody should know that the longer you wait to do something, the worse the chances of that person surviving. Every minute matters, and it was always hard to know how long someone had been down."

"Remember the mouthpieces people used to sell?" I interjected. "The ones you were supposed to carry in your glove compartment should you come across someone who needed CPR? Well intentioned, but I don't think I ever saw anybody use one. And I agree about the mouth-to-mouth. It's not something that comes naturally, with a stranger and all. And it can lead to a lot of guilt."

"What do you mean?" Shep looked over at me.

"Just like you said about getting to the scene and everybody just standing around. There's a lot of guilt with that—maybe not right away, but it will show up. Family members especially, but even strangers will wonder if they should have done something, and if they had, if that person would still be alive."

"Now it's straightforward, don't you think?" Shep said. "With the new guidelines. But I'll have to admit, at first I was skeptical that just doing chest compressions is as good as chest compressions plus artificial breathing. Makes sense, I guess, with hard compressions and movement of the chest wall. But like I said, I was skeptical."

"You weren't the only one," I agreed. "But all the studies confirm it to be true. Now the key is to make sure the public knows, so when you fall over…"

"Hey, I'm younger than you!" he objected.

"Yeah, but you eat more cheeseburgers and fries."

Shep stroked his chin and nodded. "True. You got me there."

I started writing on my chart again, but something he said earlier came to my mind. "You said it was getting harder to do the right thing, to do what needs to be done. Tell me about that."

Shep took a deep breath, blew it out, and rested his elbows on the counter of the nurses' station.

"It's the little things, I guess. Something small here—a little bigger there. New rules and regulations. And HIPAA. Always HIPAA."

There were good things that happened with HIPAA—some changes that needed to be made. But there were bad things as well—more red tape, less communication, and entire new hospital administrative departments. But I was interested in these new rules and regulations Shep was talking about.

"Tell me about some of these regulations. What's chapping you there?" He shook his head. "One of the main ones, something that really bugs us, is…well, let me just tell you what happened on a call about a month ago."

Engine 2 was barreling down Cherry Road, responding to an unknown emergency at a gas station near Winthrop University. As they pulled into the parking area, a couple of dozen people scattered, leaving a small nucleus surrounding a middle-aged man lying flat on his back.

Shep and Troy, his engineer, were the first out of the truck.

"What's the story here?" Shep asked the group.

Troy checked the man for a pulse, shook his head, and opened the medical kit.

"He was just putting gas in his car," one of the onlookers volunteered. "Just standing there. And then I heard some gurgling, and the next thing I knew he staggered over here and collapsed right where you see him."

"Has he been breathing?" Troy asked. "Any pulse?"

Shep ripped off the man's shirt, exposing his bare chest. No movement of his chest wall.

"No…I don't think so. I…we…" The onlooker hung his head and slunk back into the gathering group.

The rest of Shep's crew ran up to them, each knowing what they needed to do.

Troy attached cardiac electrodes, and Roddy positioned his large, overlapping palms over the man's sternum. He looked up at his captain. Shep nodded, and Roddy began chest compressions.

The man's color was a dusky blue, but he was warm, and Shep could feel Roddy's compressions generating a pulse in his left carotid artery.

"Any idea how long he's been down?" Shep asked the group.

Silence.

"How long has he been like this?"

"Just a couple of minutes," some faceless person ventured. "Not long. Five at the most."

Multiple sirens announced the approach of EMS units and the city police.

Shep and his team kept working, with Roddy providing 100 chest compressions per minute. Textbook.

Shep thought the man's color was improving—something must be going right.

The crowd parted, and two paramedics rushed up beside them. Two more from another unit rolled their stretcher toward the group, along with their defibrillator and other equipment.

Shep told the lead paramedic what he knew and what had happened since their arrival.

"How long has he been down?" the paramedic asked. "Any idea?"

Shep shook his head. "We've been here ten to twelve minutes. Before that, we don't know. Could have been five minutes, maybe more."

The paramedic looked at his watch. "Four thirty-two. If he's still flatline with no respiratory effort, we'll go another five minutes, max."

Troy looked at the paramedic and then at Shep. They had heard of the new directive from EMS stating that 20 minutes was the cutoff for CPR, but this was still something new, something they hadn't run into yet.

"He seems to be improving," Shep told the paramedic. "Color's better, and he's moving air. He can't be more than 40 or so, and without any kind of history, I think we should—"

"Twenty minutes, Shep," the paramedic told him. He sighed and shook his head. "That's what we have to do unless we have something overriding it from medical control. And I don't think that's going to happen, not knowing how long this guy has been down."

"Here, let me take over." One of the paramedics knelt beside Roddy and waited for him to take a break. When the engineer backed away, he resumed chest compressions.

Shep looked down at the man and watched for what seemed only seconds.

"Four thirty-seven," the lead paramedic announced. "Let's call it."

Quiet murmuring from the crowd as they backed away, got into cars, or simply walked off.

Shep stood there, staring down at the motionless figure lying in front of him.

Troy walked up beside him and said, "You think we should quit? How long has it been?"

This was something new to all of them—the "20-minute rule," some were calling it.

The lead paramedic looked over at the two firefighters, saw Shep staring at the man on the pavement, and walked over.

"I know what you're thinking, Shep. Bothers me too sometimes. But it's standard policy now, and believe me, it's something the admin guys look hard at. We've got to make sure our t's are crossed and i's dotted."

Troy pointed to the man on the ground. "You think this guy cares about your t's and i's?"

Shep turned to his crewmate. "Troy, take it easy."

The younger firefighter glared at the paramedic, spun around, and stormed away.

"We're all on the same team," Shep told the paramedic. "And we're all trying to do the right thing. But it seems like it's getting tougher to do that."

The paramedic sighed, shook his head, and walked away.

I studied Shep's face for a moment. It had been a month, and this was still bothering him. I understood. We were facing some of the same things in the ER.

"Bean counters," he murmured. "More and more bean counters looking over our shoulders at everything we do. You just gotta hope they're counting the right beans. But it doesn't seem so, at least not to me. I'm just glad there weren't any bean counters at the grocery store at the beach two weeks ago."

Then he told me about Ned Ryder.

"I'm going to run down to the store and work on this grocery list," Shep called to his wife. Shep, Cathy, and their two daughters, Annie and Kelsy, had just arrived at their Surfside condo for a long weekend getaway.

"The girls want to get in a swim before dinner," Cathy answered, "so that will work out just fine."

Shep grabbed the car keys and headed downstairs. Five minutes later, he was in the local Publix supermarket, staring at the list in his hand and trying to decide where to start.

Butter, eggs, milk.

As in most grocery stores, the dairy department was in the back-left corner of the building. He stuffed the list in his pocket and started in that direction.

Shep passed a half-dozen aisles. He came to one where he noticed ten or twelve people huddled together, staring at something on the floor.

Curious, he made a detour toward the group and was immediately stopped by one of the store's employees.

"Sorry, but you'll need to go the other way," the middle-aged man told him.

"What's going on?" Shep looked beyond him, trying to glimpse the center of this activity.

"I'm the store manager, sir, and if you'll just give us some room." He pointed over Shep's shoulder.

"Fine," the firefighter said, not looking at him. Without any hesitation, Shep stepped past the manager and hurried down the aisle.

"Excuse me." Shep's voice was firm, authoritative. "Let me get by, please."

The people in front of him turned toward his voice and backed out of his way.

Now he could clearly see the cause of their concern. Lying on his back in the middle of the aisle was a young man, maybe in his thirties. His eyes were glazed and staring at the ceiling. And he wasn't breathing. Shep rushed to his side and knelt. Clutched in the man's left hand was a grocery list.

"Someone call 911," Shep said to the group.

The manager had followed Shep down the aisle. He leaned over and put a hand on the firefighter's shoulder. "Sir, if you'll—"

"You can help by calling 911," Shep told him. "And have these people back up and give me some room."

The manager didn't need to be told twice. He reached for his cell phone and motioned for the people to move away.

"Did anyone see what happened?" Shep asked as he positioned the man squarely on his back and felt for a pulse.

"I was down there getting some mayonnaise," an elderly woman responded, pointing to the other end of the aisle. "I heard a funny noise and turned around just in time to see him clutch his chest and kneel down. Then he fell over."

"How long ago was that?" Shep didn't look at her as he started chest compressions.

"Four minutes—five, maybe."

"Has anybody done CPR?" he asked the group, regrettably knowing the answer.

Silence.

"EMS is on the way," the manager said from behind him. "Ten minutes, they think. And we think his name is Ned Ryder—one of the locals."

They got there in nine. Shep kept up his compressions and was sweating when the two paramedics arrived.

"Here, let me take over," one of them said to the firefighter. "Looks like you know what you're doing. Can you tell us what happened here?"

Shep rocked back on his heels and planted his hands on his thighs. He was about to speak when he noticed two young girls—six or eight years old—standing in the middle of the onlookers and staring at the body on the floor.

Shep got the attention of a woman in the crowd and motioned with his head to the children.

"Should probably get them away from this," he whispered to her. "Would you mind doing that?"

The woman leaned close to Shep and said, "I think those are his daughters."

Within minutes, Ned Ryder had an IV started, an endotracheal tube in place, EKG electrodes fastened to his chest…and no pulse.

They continued working, and after a few minutes, Shep slid forward and took over the chest compressions.

Still no pulse, and no spontaneous respirations.

"Probably need to call this," one of the paramedics said quietly. "Been at least 20, maybe 30 minutes."

Sweat was pouring down Shep's forehead again. He glanced over at the two girls—staring at *him* now.

The question in Shep's mind was, how long had Ned been down before he got there? He knew they had been providing effective CPR. It was just a matter of—

"Check the monitor," the paramedic said, pointing to the small screen.

Shep's eyes darted to the defibrillator, just in time to see one…two purposeful blips. They slid past and were gone. Flatline.

A few minutes more, and a few more intermittent blips. His heart was trying, and it was the least—

The paramedic put a hand on Shep's shoulder. "I think we need to call it."

Shep looked at the lifeless man and then at his daughters.

"Let's get him loaded and to the hospital," he said between labored breaths. "I'm not going to stop these compressions until we get him to the ER."

The paramedics looked at each other and then at the firefighter. "Okay."

Just as they pulled up to the ambulance entrance of the ER, there was a burst of activity on the monitor. Shep checked for a pulse over Ned's carotid artery and thought he felt something—something faint, but still something.

The back doors of the ambulance opened, and a group of ER nurses and techs stood waiting. "Let's get him into Cardiac!"

Shep paused, took a deep breath, and was silent.

I waited for as long as I could. "Well, what happened to Ned Ryder? Did he make it?"

He looked over at me, and nothing in his face or eyes betrayed what was to follow.

"Let me just say that two days ago we had some visitors at the station. This man walks in with his wife and two daughters. They ask for me, and he walks up, shakes my hand, and says, 'Hi. I'm Ned Ryder.'"

I stared at him, not knowing what to say.

Finally, I mumbled something about his doing a good job and persevering and about how thankful I knew they were that he happened to be at the store at that moment.

Shep picked up his clipboard, smiled at me, and walked out of the ER.

Thank God for Shep Stevens—and for all the men and women like him.

If you do the right thing,
you won't go wrong.

ANONYMOUS

19

What's in the Well Comes Up in the Bucket

Roger Schroeder had done it. He had finally achieved his dream of becoming a full-fledged police officer and was sitting in the call room, waiting for morning report. His *first* morning report.

Chief Dan Carothers had called him a week earlier and offered him a job. Then his longtime friend, Charlie Whitesell, called too, welcoming him to the force. Now here he sat—uniform spotless and pressed, badge pinned proudly to his chest, and service weapon holstered at his waist. He was ready, but it hadn't come easily.

Roger finished high school with honors and soon announced his intention to pursue a career in law enforcement. This was something he had wanted since grade school—something he had never second-guessed.

That job, the second-guessing part, had been handled by his father. He never thought Roger was serious about becoming a police officer and never thought it necessary to discourage his son. But when Roger announced his plans, his father put his foot down and insisted on a different course for his son's life. Jack Schroeder was a successful banker, and he was determined that his son would pursue a career in business.

"I went to Furman, your mother went to Furman, two of your grandparents went to Furman, and that's where you will go. Period."

Two years after that declaration, Roger came home following the completion of his sophomore year at Furman University. He handed his father the letter declaring his fourth consecutive inclusion on the Dean's List and told him he wasn't going back.

There was no explosion, no expletive-filled rant, no berating of his son. Jack Schroeder relented. He knew Roger had tried—that he had complied with his directive to forgo law enforcement and attend Furman. He finally came to understand and accept Roger's dreams and passion. Roger's mother had been instrumental in that transformation. She knew her son and was gentle yet constant in her efforts to convince her husband. In the end, Jack Schroeder became his son's biggest supporter.

Eighteen months and hundreds of calls after that first morning report, Roger received an award for his response to a difficult and dangerous situation. His actions averted the deaths of at least two people and further earned him the respect of the other officers and staff in the department. Roger Schroeder was doing what he was meant to do, and he knew it. But a change was taking place. Dark tentacles were working their way into Roger's heart. And no one, not even Roger, would have ever predicted or even imagined the road he was traveling.

"All units, respond to a 10-50—intersection of Maplewood and State Street. Possible injuries."

Roger looked at his partner, Hutch Anderson, and nodded. They were nearby—minutes away from the usually quiet intersection in what had become a challenging part of town.

Lights, siren, and they were on the way. Hutch was in the passenger seat. He radioed Dispatch, telling them they were en route.

"Funny place for a wreck," Hutch offered. "Middle of the day and not much traffic over there."

They were the first unit to arrive, and Roger slowed as the patrol car approached a confusing scene. The houses in this neighborhood had slowly drifted into disrepair—tilted or missing shutters, weed-infested yards, and low, once-proud stone walls that now crumbled into piles of rubble. A few dozen people meandered down broken sidewalks toward a late-model SUV that was wrapped around a splintered and slanting telephone pole. No one seemed very excited.

Roger and Hutch jumped out of their car and ran toward the heap of twisted metal and plastic.

EMS 2 screamed into the middle of the intersection and came to an abrupt stop. Two paramedics bolted from the ambulance and raced toward the police officers.

Roger was the first to reach the SUV. The driver, Bernadette Green, stood on the other side and wiped a stream of blood from her forehead. She was unstable and rocked from side to side.

Head injury. I need to get her down before she falls.

The officer rushed to her, put his arms around her shoulders, and flinched. She smelled of cigarettes and cheap wine. There was no significant head injury. She was just dead drunk at eleven in the morning.

One of the paramedics joined him and recoiled when he got close to the woman's face—and breath.

"Let's get her on the stretcher," he said, motioning to his partner.

The woman took two wobbly steps toward the stretcher, stumbled, and grabbed Roger around the neck.

"Mama!"

A little girl—five or six years old—stepped into view from behind the woman. She had hidden herself, clutching the legs of her teetering mother. The girl was frightened but unscathed, and Hutch gently guided her to the side of the stretcher, where her mother now reclined.

The little girl looked up and whimpered.

"Come on, July," the woman mumbled. "Be still and hush your mouth."

The child hung her head and followed the stretcher to the back of the ambulance.

"Where's April?" the woman muttered again. "Go find your sister and tell her to come on."

April? Is there another child out here somewhere?

Roger glanced around at the crowd of people. No small children. He rushed over to the folded SUV and looked through the driver's window. Nothing.

Then he stiffened, every muscle frozen. A tiny, shoeless foot was on the backseat floor, covered in blood—the body buried under a couple of jackets and fast-food wrappers.

"I need some help!" Roger rushed to the other side of the vehicle and struggled with the door. Dented and partially pinned to the pole, it finally yielded.

April, three years old, was dead—killed instantly when her unbelted body was tossed around the backseat at the point of collision.

Investigators later estimated a rate of speed exceeding 70 miles per hour. Bernadette never braked the SUV and probably never saw the light or the pole. She had a couple of pieces of glass in her forehead, but that was it. She was quickly released to the custody of the police. July was in the custody of the state's department of social services. This wasn't the first time Bernadette had acted irresponsibly with her children. And except for that one time on the stretcher, she never again asked about April.

A week later, Roger and Hutch were finishing up their evening shift.

"What ya think?" Hutch asked. "It's ten thirty. Head back to the station?"

Before Roger could say anything, Dispatch answered Hutch's question.

"All units respond to 144 Davis Street. Domestic dispute."

"Guess not," Hutch mumbled.

It had been a long day, and they were both tired. Hopefully this would be a simple he-said, she-said argument, and it could be quickly handled. But they both knew domestic disturbances could rapidly turn dangerous and deadly.

Hutch radioed their location—five minutes away—and the team was given the assignment. They turned off Charlotte Avenue and headed toward Davis Street.

Hutch turned to Roger and studied his partner for a moment.

"You're still bothered by that little girl last week, aren't you?"

Roger tightened his grip on the steering wheel and nodded. He and his wife, Melanie, had been trying for two years to become pregnant. Those dark and stressful months had only brought three miscarriages and a lot of tears.

"I just don't understand how a mother with two girls—"

"There it is," Hutch interrupted, pointing to a house on their right. "144 Davis."

Thirty-four-year-old Ray Jagger was walking out of the front door as the two officers approached.

"Who called you guys?" he huffed. "Some nosy neighbor?"

It *had* been a "nosy" neighbor, concerned for the safety of this man's wife. The officers didn't respond to his question.

A curtain in the window on the left of the doorway fluttered, and Roger caught a glimpse of a woman—wide-eyed and bruised.

"Can we have a word with you and your wife?" he asked.

"Martha? Sure. Let me see your warrant and I'll be glad to talk with you."

The two officers stood there, staring at this angry man.

A tense moment passed. Ray shook his head and spat on the front porch.

"That's what I thought. I'm outta here."

He stepped off the porch, roughly brushing Hutch's arm as he passed.

They looked at each other, helpless to stop the man. Roger took a few steps toward the front door and knocked.

Martha Jagger cracked it open and peered at the two men.

"Yes, can I…" She lowered her head and sobbed.

"Can we come in for a minute, ma'am?" Roger asked quietly. "We'd like to talk with you."

They sat in the living room—the two policemen on the sofa and Martha huddled in a recliner, her knees drawn up to her chest. The bruises on her face were older and of different ages, but her lower lip was fresh—puffy and bleeding.

"I know it's my fault," she stammered. "He's a good man, and he works hard."

"A good man?" Hutch leaned toward her.

Roger put a hand on his partner's forearm.

"Mrs. Jagger," he said quietly, "we're here to help. And there are people in the community who can help as well. I don't think you're safe here."

It was hopeless. Martha refused to go with the officers or even file a complaint.

"It's my fault," she lamented, getting up out of the chair and walking to the door. "I'll try to do better."

On the way back to the station, Hutch wrote up their report. "I don't understand it. That guy beats her and should be locked up. But what can we do if she won't press charges?"

"I don't know," Roger said, his voice low and troubled. "I feel like I should have done more. I should have insisted she come with us or something."

"Hey, we did all we could. *You* did all you could."

Three days later, a team of Rock Hill police officers responded to a call. "Shots fired—144 Davis Street." Martha Jagger was dead.

Hutch took the news hard, but Roger didn't say a word. Not until he walked into Chief Carothers's office and turned in his badge and service weapon.

"Son," Jack said to his boy, "I want you to give this some thought. Take some time before you decide anything final. You've worked hard to get where you are, and I'm proud of what you've accomplished. You're a good police officer, and we all need people like you—people who care. Things happen, bad things, and you have to deal with them the best you can."

His mother didn't talk about what had broken him down, about what had broken his spirit. She just prayed for her son.

Roger stopped taking calls from Hutch and Charlie Whitesell. Even from Chief Carothers. He had made up his mind and come to believe his lifelong dream of becoming a police officer had just been a fantasy— the wild and foolish illusion of an eight-year-old boy.

Six months passed, and he was working at Home Depot, waiting to start the next semester at Furman. He would be a banker, just like his father.

"See you guys later," he called to a couple of friends walking with him through the parking lot of the orange-fronted store. He had finished his shift and was headed home.

Roger cranked his car and glanced at the gas gauge. Almost empty.

He pulled onto the highway and headed toward the BP station, a half mile away.

It was mid-February and cold. He shivered and waited for the car's heater to wake up.

He shivered again at the pump, stomping his feet and rubbing his hands together while the gallons clicked their way into his tank.

Finished, he screwed the gas cap back in place. He put a hand on the door latch and half opened the door. Something caused him to stop, and he decided to step into the station and get something to drink and some peanuts.

He walked into the store and knew something was wrong. The middle-aged clerk stood behind the counter, his hands by his side and his saucer-sized eyes unblinking. His head turned toward Roger and then back to the aisle facing him. Roger stopped in the doorway, his body tense. Something wasn't—

A masked figure stepped out of the aisle and into full view. Without a word, the man pointed his .38 at Roger and motioned him into the store.

Every piece of Roger's police training flashed through his mind. His eyes flitted around the space in front of him. His brain took it all in, and he made a plan.

He moved slowly toward the counter, his hands raised to shoulder level.

"That's far enough," the muffled voice warned.

Roger stopped. He was close to the man now—maybe five feet. And he could see behind the counter. The clerk stood statue-like—not moving, maybe not breathing. On the floor by the clerk's feet, Roger saw a pool of blood—and two legs. He stared, his face flushed and his heart pounding in his chest. One of the feet moved, just a little, and Roger vaulted into the air, landing on top of the armed robber.

"He saved our lives!"

The clerk stood beside the EMS stretcher with one hand on his son's shoulder. With the other, he pointed at Roger Schroeder.

He ran around the stretcher and grabbed and shook Roger's hand for the umpteenth time. "Thank you! You saved my son!"

The teenage boy lay with IVs in both arms and a bullet in his belly. He would live, thanks to Roger's quick thinking and quicker actions.

Hutch was standing beside his ex-partner.

"You done good," he beamed. "I'm proud of you."

Roger, stilled flushed with the last surges of adrenaline, took a deep breath and stood there.

Hutch leaned close and quietly said, "You know, Roger, this is what you were born to do."

Six months later, Furman began its fall semester. Eighty miles away, a dispatcher sat in her office and spoke into the radio.

"All units respond. Breaking and entering at 359 Clyde Street."

Hutch looked at Roger. "Let's go."

One road leads home
and a thousand roads lead into the wilderness.

C.S. Lewis

20

Cynthia

L ee Keller was standing beside me at the nurses' station when the stretcher of EMS 3 rolled through the ambulance entrance doors. "This is the overdose we called in," one of the paramedics told the triage nurse. "Still want her in the Cardiac room?"

The nurse looked at the 22-year-old somnolent woman. "Still no idea what she took?"

The paramedic shook his head. "Her friends took off when we got there, and there's no family in the house. Couldn't find any pill bottles or evidence of any drugs. The call came in as an overdose with unknown medication." He glanced at his unresponsive patient. "And you can tell she hasn't been much help. Stable though, with good vital signs. We'll take her to Cardiac."

They rolled past us down the hallway, and I looked at Lee. I knew what he was going to say before he said it.

"Cynthia Morgan."

The first overdose Lee ever worked as a Rock Hill police officer was in response to a 911 call for an "unknown emergency." He arrived at the address just as an EMS unit was pulling up. He found himself in front of a large, stately home in one of the most prestigious neighborhoods in the city.

"Any idea what's going on?" one of the paramedics asked. He was walking alongside Lee as they approached the enormous hand-carved mahogany front door.

"I know about as much as you guys do. 'Unknown emergency' is all we have."

The door flew open, and a middle-aged woman appeared before them. She was dressed in a bathrobe, and her wet hair was wrapped in a towel.

"Hurry, please! She's upstairs!"

She spun around and retreated up the winding staircase.

Lee looked at the paramedic, and they both took off after the retreating woman. She turned a corner on the landing and disappeared into a bedroom.

There, passed out on the bed, was a teenage girl.

"This is my daughter," the woman told them. "And we think she took an overdose of one of my husband's pills. I have no idea why she would have tried to hurt herself. Cynthia has everything going for her and…I just don't understand."

Cynthia was an 18-year-old high school senior and would be graduating in two weeks. She did have everything going for her. Valedictorian of her class, cheerleader, star soccer player, full scholarship to Clemson, solid friends, and a supportive family.

"Here, this is what she took."

Her mother handed a half-empty medicine bottle to the paramedic. He rolled it over in his hand, studying the label.

"Hmm…is this the only medicine she might have taken?"

"That's the only one that has anything missing. She was in her room when I got into the shower. I found her like this and immediately called 911. I saw this pill bottle beside her bed and went into our room to see if anything else might be missing. Everything else is in the medicine cabinet and hasn't been disturbed. I don't know how she got this bottle or when, but she probably took seven or eight of the capsules."

The paramedic held the bottle so Lee could read the label.

Prevacid. A benign stomach medication.

Lee cocked his head at the paramedic and raised one eyebrow.

The paramedic stepped to the side of the bed and laid his hand on Cynthia's shoulder. Lee thought he saw her eyelids squint a little.

"Cynthia, I think you're going to be okay. And when you're ready to talk about this, we'll be ready to listen."

It took a little more than 15 minutes, but the young woman miraculously woke up, examined her surroundings, and asked her mother, "What in the world is going on?"

That was the day bad things started for Cynthia Morgan. Her parents weren't interested in taking her to the hospital for any sort of psychiatric examination. The paramedic had explained that while there was no immediate physical danger, this sort of behavior was frequently symptomatic of underlying emotional problems—some potentially very serious.

"We'll take her to our family doctor in a few days," her mother responded. "Thanks for your concern, but we'll be fine."

They didn't visit their doctor in a few days—or any other counselor. Hindsight is always 20/20, and this first episode had been an initial whimper for help. Cynthia was becoming depressed under the pressure of performing well in academics and sports, and the unknowns of college only added to her stressors.

A few months passed, and one weekend her parents got a call from the Clemson infirmary. Cynthia had taken another overdose of an unknown medicine, this time with a significant amount of alcohol. She spent three weeks at home, at the end of which she convinced her parents she was fine and ready to go back to school.

She dropped out of college five months later and moved back in with her mother and father.

Cynthia stopped taking care of herself, and the promising young high school senior was now unkempt, listless, and possessed of a disturbing and vacant stare.

We saw her in the ER over the next few years—nothing major or life-threatening, but always something that stemmed from her unhappiness and deep-seated depression. For whatever reason, her parents seemed more embarrassed by her condition than concerned for her well-being or maybe even her life. We mentioned having one of the staff counselors talk with her, but they weren't interested, and Cynthia wasn't going to get into an argument with her parents or risk the chance of embarrassing them. Nothing ever came of those conversations, but something was going to give, and it wasn't going to be good.

That "something" occurred two weeks before Christmas.

It was another 911 call, this one for the police, regarding "a woman with a gun, threatening to hurt herself." The address was off one of the city's main thoroughfares, in an apartment complex. Lee Keller and his partner took the call.

The apartment was on the second floor of the building, and when the officers got to the scene, four or five young people were standing outside the open door of the apartment. They cleared an opening as Lee and his partner approached.

Inside they found a young man pointing to a bedroom just off the living area. The door was open, and they could hear a young woman pleading.

"Cynthia, put that down. You know you don't want to hurt yourself. Think about your mother and father."

Lee leaned close to his partner and whispered. "Stay out of sight for a minute. We don't want her to feel outnumbered and frightened. I'll see what's going on."

He walked into the room and found Cynthia Morgan sitting bolt upright on the edge of the bed, holding a small-caliber revolver to her right temple.

"Oh, thank heaven, officer," her friend sighed. She was standing in front of the dresser, at least ten feet from Cynthia. "Maybe you can talk some sense into her."

Lee knew Cynthia from many 911 calls, and he knew the look in her eye. There was little chance of talking any sense into Cynthia, but he was going to try.

"Your friend's right." His speech was measured and calm. "You don't want to hurt yourself. We don't want you to hurt yourself. Look." He slowly raised his empty hands in the air. "I just want to talk with you."

For the first time, he realized his predicament. A shiver of fear passed over him but then was gone. He was standing in front of an armed and disturbed young woman, completely defenseless. If she turned her weapon on him, he would have no time to respond. Just like Cynthia's friend, he was at least ten feet from the young woman.

He didn't think she would try to harm him. Still…

"Let's talk about this, okay? Tell me what's so bad right now."

Cynthia's eyes traveled to her friend and back to Lee. She sighed but didn't move.

"It's too late."

The words hung in the air like a toxic cloud. There was no life in her voice. No emotion. No hope.

"It's never too late, Cynthia. There's always—"

The gunshot was deafening, and then the screaming. Cynthia collapsed on the floor, and her friend ran from the room.

Lee's partner raced into the bedroom, service weapon drawn.

"Oh my God!"

EMS 3 came screaming up to the ambulance entrance. A moment later the doors burst open, and the stretcher carrying Cynthia Morgan barreled down the hallway and toward Major Trauma.

"Gunshot wound to the head!" the paramedic shouted as he passed the nurses' station. "Stable blood pressure and pulse. She's breathing but unresponsive."

I followed them into Trauma and turned to face the unit secretary. "Get X-ray down here, and lab. And we'll need respiratory therapy."

I was pulling the door closed and noticed Lee Keller standing in the hallway. His eyes were fixed on mine—wide open and unblinking. His face was drained of any color. The door closed, and we went to work, futile as that might be.

That was three years ago, and Lee and I were thinking of the same person. Cynthia Morgan. And of how her dark journey began with an overdose, a cry for help.

"I'll never forget that day," Lee sighed. "Standing in that room with her, trying to talk her down, and then suddenly the gunshot ringing in my ears. Nothing I could do about it."

"I can only imagine, Lee." But I really couldn't—not the stress of that moment or the gun going off. Not the sense of failure that must have immediately engulfed the young police officer.

"And then when you came out of Major Trauma." He stopped and pointed at the doorway. "The look on your face…I didn't know what to think."

"I didn't know what to think either," I agreed. "There was no earthly explanation for what happened."

"You know, I didn't believe you, not at first. It was only when you took me into Trauma and I saw her sitting up and talking. I still can't believe what happened."

The moment came flashing back to my mind, and I felt the same sense of disbelief and wonder I had experienced then. In a chaotic flurry of activity, we tried to stabilize Cynthia. Every gunshot wound to the head I had ever treated ultimately proved to be fatal—some lasted moments, and some days or even weeks. But they were always fatal.

The entrance wound was easily identified over her right temple, and I looked for an exit wound. Lee had told me the weapon was a small-caliber pistol, so it might not have had the power to penetrate both sides of her skull. One side would be enough, with the projectile tumbling and destroying the brain matter within.

I was unable to find any evidence of an exit wound, but something was unusual. Something wasn't quite right when I examined the back of her head. And then she began to blink. Her pupils had been equal—an unexpected good sign—and I thought they might have reacted to the beam of my penlight. But the room was bright, and it was hard to tell for sure.

"Did you see that?" one of the nurses observed. "She blinked when you picked up her head."

I reached down and lightly stroked the lashes of her left eye. Both eyes squinted, and her right hand came off the stretcher a few inches.

The nurse looked at me, her own eyes squinting. I was puzzled too, and I reexamined the back of Cynthia's head. There was a track of some sort—almost a burrow—beginning at the entrance wound, extending around her posterior skull, and ending just above her right ear.

"What in the…"

"What is it, Dr. Lesslie?"

"There's a bullet here." I pointed at the end of the track and traced the contours of what had to be a metal slug. "I don't think it ever penetrated her—"

And then Cynthia Morgan sat up and looked around the room.

"I really didn't believe it until you showed me her X-rays, Doc. There was that tiny ding on the outside of her skull bone, at her right temple, and then nothing else. The bullet had somehow tracked around her head, just under the skin, finally coming to rest above her left ear. Have you ever heard of anything like that happening before?"

"Only in the movies," I told him. "And maybe not even then. Who would believe it?"

But we had both seen it, and we both believed. More miraculous than that, though, was the change the whole thing brought about in Cynthia. It was as if a switch in her mind had flipped when that gun went off. She had been admitted to the hospital—not so much for her medical condition as for her psychiatric situation and determined suicide attempt. And that's when things began to change—both for her and for her parents. The transformation was unexplainable and complete. She had a lot of work to do, but with the help of her mother and father and a capable Christian counselor, she was able to right her ship and find a new direction. We learned she went on to finish Clemson—graduating with honors—and was now enrolled in nursing school. Her mother thought she might want to work in the ER someday. Full circle.

"Yeah, only in the movies," Lee echoed. "It must have been the angle she was holding that gun. Just misdirected enough to send that bullet on a tangent. But when I saw her in that bedroom, holding the gun, I remember thinking she knew what she was doing—pointing it at ninety degrees—right at her brain."

I nodded and looked at Lee. "We both know what happened then."

"We both know what?" He cocked his head.

"Cynthia told me what happened right before she pulled the trigger. You must have jumped across the room and jarred her hand just a little. That's what she felt, right before the impact caused her to lose consciousness. You saved that girl's life, and she knows it."

Lee stared at me, his mouth open.

A moment passed, and he didn't utter a word.

"What is it, Lee? What's the matter?"

"We've never talked about this before, Doc. I was standing ten feet away, and that gun went off before I could do anything."

He was silent again. And then, "I never touched her."

Don't be afraid.
Just stand still and watch the LORD rescue you today.
EXODUS 14:13 NLT

21

The Choice

"So, what do you want to be when you grow up?"

This was a reasonable question from one eight-year-old to another. Especially if they were best friends. When Jimmy Anderson didn't immediately answer, Todd Bryant repeated his question.

"Come on, Jimmy, what do you want to be?"

Jimmy had heard the question. He was thinking.

He looked squarely at Todd. "I want to be a fireman."

"No, really. Everybody says that. What do you *really* want to be?" Todd persisted.

"A fireman. Really. My Uncle Bill is a fireman in Atlanta, and what he does is pretty crazy. He's not afraid of anything, and he saves people's lives. That's what I want to do."

Jimmy swung his legs over the edge of the weathered dock. It was almost noon, and the boys were fishing in the Andersons' farm pond. "A fireman," he mused. "I think that'd be fun."

Something tugged on his float but then was gone.

"What about you?" Jimmy looked at his friend. "Still wanna be a pro basketball player?"

Todd shook his head. "I'm gonna be too short, like my daddy. Be nice though, traveling and making all that money. But I doubt it."

He reeled in his line and pulled the float and hook out of the water.

"Dadgummit! Cleaned me again! I'm gonna catch that bass if I have to stay here all day."

"Well, that ain't gonna happen. We only got two more crickets, so you'd better make 'em count. But go on and tell me. If you're not gonna be a basketball player, what else do you want to do?"

Todd carefully placed the protesting cricket on his hook and tossed it into the water.

"I thought about bein' a doctor, but you have to go to school for about 50 years, and then you have to stay inside all the time. So I'm sorta leaning toward being a para…a para…"

"A paramedic?" Jimmy said. "You mean ridin' with the ambulance and stuff like that? The EMS? That'd be pretty cool." He paused and chuckled.

"What's so funny about that?" Todd punched his friend on the arm.

"It's just that wouldn't it be strange if we called 911 someday and you showed up at the door? I think everyone would take off runnin'."

"About as fast as if *you* showed up at a fire."

It was Jimmy's turn to punch Todd's arm.

"Dadgummit! That bass cleaned my bait again!"

Sixteen years went by, and both boys achieved their dreams. Jimmy had become a fireman, quickly climbing the ladder and becoming one of the leaders of his engine unit. He was known for being smart, quick, and brave. Not foolhardy, but not hesitating to do what needed to be done.

Todd had finished EMT and paramedic school with honors, and he was now the lead paramedic on EMS 1, the premier unit in town—and the busiest.

They had remained close friends, married their high school sweethearts, and lived in the same city. They still went fishing together, and Todd still frequently struggled with keeping a cricket on his hook.

When 911 calls came in to the central dispatcher, all available first responders were sent to the scene. This included the police, EMS, and the fire department. It might be a heart attack, fire, auto accident, or unknown medical emergency. It was as first responders that Todd and

Jimmy occasionally joined forces in the field or on the highway. And it was a source of competition for the two friends.

"You guys are a little slow today, aren't you, Todd?" Jimmy poked his friend one afternoon.

He and his engine unit had arrived at the scene of a logging-truck accident moments before EMS 1 screamed up to the flaming hunk of twisted metal lying on its side in the ditch beside Highway 5. The driver had escaped serious injury and had narrowly missed a pickup truck and its three passengers when he lost control taking a sharp turn.

"They need to fix this stretch of highway." Todd waved his hand at the narrow, curved ribbon of asphalt. "Had another trucker out here two weeks ago with the same thing—lost control of his rig, and logs were everywhere. Cab was completely burned out."

"Seems to me we beat you to that one too," Jimmy ribbed him. "Maybe you guys need some driving lessons or a faster ambulance. It's getting to be embarrassing to always beat you to the scene."

Regardless of who arrived first, the two young men were professionals, and they respected each other and knew their roles. If they were responding to the victim of a heart attack and Jimmy and his crew were the first to arrive, they started CPR but quickly yielded to the paramedics. And if it was a fire or if an emergency extrication was needed, the firefighters called the shots. That's the way it worked, and that's the way lives were saved. But not every life was saved.

"All available units respond. Unknown medical emergency, 316 Cranford Road. Police en route."

Todd looked at his partner. "Cranford Road. This can't be good."

Cranford was known for its less than upright citizenry. Like many areas in our larger cities, this had once been a neighborhood of hardworking families, but it was now the haven of drug dealers and users. Many of the dwellings had fallen into disrepair and were now crack houses.

"Glad the police are going to be there. We might need them."

EMS 1 had responded to a call on Cranford Road a few weeks earlier, and Todd's young partner, Steve Winn, had received some uncomfortable but necessary education. It seems that ambulances are not always welcome in certain neighborhoods, and theirs had been greeted with a brick thrown through the front windshield and a bullet hole in the back door. They didn't notice the bullet hole for a couple of days, and when Steve saw it, his face turned a pasty white and he almost quit on the spot.

"I had the same reaction the first time it happened to me," Todd told him. "Don't know what makes people do that kind of thing. We're out there just trying to help, but some folks are plain mean or crazy or both. But it doesn't happen very often. You just need to be careful. And you need to hope the police are at the scene when you get there."

The flashing blue lights of three police cruisers greeted them as they drove up to the address on Cranford Road. Todd glanced into his side mirror and saw Jimmy's engine unit pulling up right behind them. He chuckled.

Steve grabbed his medical kit and jumped out of the ambulance. Todd followed, waving at Jimmy as he jogged toward them.

"What you got?"

"Don't know yet," Todd answered.

"Somebody called in an overdose." One of the police officers walked over and spoke to the men. He casually motioned behind him with a thumb. "Two guys in the house, but I don't think they could have called it in. One's unresponsive and the other can barely talk. Looks like heroin, so be careful of the needles. There's a bunch lying all over the place. Must have had quite a party for a couple of days. And the unresponsive one is Slick Perkins."

Todd glanced at Jimmy and shook his head.

"What?" Steve looked at the two men. "Who is Slick Perkins? You know him?"

Every veteran on the police force, EMS, and the fire department knew Slick Perkins. In and out of jail, in and out of the hospital. He was a bad actor in spite of multiple attempts to get him some help. He had been raised by his grandparents until they had to give up.

"Anybody else in the building?" Jimmy was moving toward the house, walking beside Todd and Steve. "Don't want any surprises. You know how these guys can get."

"You're right," the police officer agreed. "And no, we checked it out. Nobody else inside. Just a couple of curious neighbors nosing around outside."

He nodded in the direction of the house next door. Four or five young men were huddled in the doorway, leaning haphazardly and staring at the flashing lights and uniformed commotion.

"One of my guys is in there, and we'll maintain a perimeter while you do your work."

"Thanks," Steve said. Todd and Jimmy heard the relief in Steve's voice and understood.

The front porch was lit by a single bulb dangling from twisted and frayed wires.

"That's a violation for sure," Jimmy chuckled.

"Not going to be the only violation in this place," Todd added.

A police officer was standing in what had once been the living room but was now a repository for trash, old blankets, and empty cans of assorted food. He was writing on his notepad and looked up at the three men as they entered.

"Bedroom, right over there." He pointed to a doorway in the right-hand side of the room. A dim light guided their way.

"What's that smell?" Steve waved the air in front of his nose.

"Could be anything," Jimmy answered. "No plumbing in most of these houses now, so I've got a pretty good idea."

"Man, why would someone live like this?"

"I'm not sure I'd call it living." Todd shook his head. They reached the doorway and stopped. "See what I mean?"

The floor of the small room was littered with trash, old pizza boxes, empty wine bottles, and drug paraphernalia.

"Remember what the officer said, Steve. Watch out for the needles. This place screams of hepatitis C."

"And HIV," Jimmy added.

A slender man of indeterminate age sat on the floor in the far corner of the room, leaning against the water-stained wall. He was shoeless but wore dirty and mismatched athletic socks. His great toes protruded through worn tips. His head lolled to one side, and his eyes opened as the men walked in. There was a meager attempt at focusing his gaze, but he failed, and his eyes rolled toward the ceiling behind half-closed lids.

"I'll check on that one." Steve motioned to the corner of the room and walked toward him, carefully picking his way through the jumbled mess on the floor.

Todd and Jimmy hurried over to another man, this one lying on a filthy gray blanket. It was Slick Perkins. His legs were askew, and a homemade tourniquet was around his left upper arm. A needle jutted from a swollen vein in his elbow.

"Let's start by getting rid of this." Jimmy reached down and removed the syringe.

"Don't release the tourniquet yet," Todd advised. "We'll give it a couple of minutes, once I get an IV started. We don't want to suddenly release a bolus of who-knows-what. How about checking his pulse and blood pressure?"

The two men worked seamlessly, evaluating and stabilizing the unconscious and critical patient.

"BP is 130 over 90." Jimmy removed the stethoscope from his ears. "And his heart rate is 110 but regular."

"That's good. I've about got this IV started, and then we'll give him some Narcan."

"That should make him happy," Jimmy chuckled.

Narcon—naloxone—was the antidote for a heroin overdose. It would rapidly reverse the effects of the drug and quickly awaken this unresponsive man…unless there was something else on board.

Jimmy was right about making him happy. Many drug users weren't thrilled with the idea of being given a medication that reversed the effects of their cherished, drug-induced euphoria, even if it meant saving their life. He and Todd had seen their share of people aroused from an opiate-induced stupor only to start fighting with their rescuers. Hard to figure.

"This guy looks okay," Steve called out from the corner of the room. "Vital signs are fine, and there's no evidence of any trauma. I'll get a line started and then bring in our stretcher. EMS 3 should be here any minute, and they can give us a hand with your guy."

"Good work," Todd said to his partner. Then to Jimmy, "Hold on to him. I'm going to push an amp of Narcan."

Todd emptied the syringe of medication into the IV in Slick's left wrist and waited. At first there was no response. Jimmy knelt on the other side of Slick and held his arms on the floor.

Half a minute passed, and Slick slowly opened his eyes. He looked around the room and then at the two men hovering over him. He muttered something unintelligible and closed his eyes again.

"Should be okay," Todd said, rocking back on his heels. "I'll take it from here. How about seeing if EMS 3 is here yet, and ask them to bring their stretcher? We need to get him loaded and to the ER."

Jimmy was in the doorway when he heard it. Scuffling and a mumbled grunt. He spun around and saw Slick Perkins—eyes wide-open—reach beneath him with his right hand and brandish a flashing blade. With lightning speed, he made a single, fluid motion and stabbed Todd in the exposed left side of his neck. Just as quickly, Slick's arm fell to the floor, and he closed his eyes. The bloody knife clattered across the floor, coming to rest against a pile of discarded clothes.

Todd grabbed his neck and looked at Jimmy. Anderson was racing to his stricken friend, calling as loudly as he could for help. Steve bolted into the room behind him just as Todd collapsed and fell over the recumbent body of Slick Perkins. Blood spurted from the wound over the paramedic's carotid, and his life drained onto the floor of 316 Cranford Road.

There was nothing they could do. Todd bled out in a matter of minutes in spite of Jimmy's effort to staunch the bleeding with as much pressure as he could muster. Slick had managed to completely sever the carotid artery, with the cut ends retracting away from the wound, pumping freely.

It was over. And Todd Bryant was dead.

Jimmy thought long and hard about resigning from the fire department after that afternoon. All of his life, he had known with absolute certainty that he and Todd were invincible—much more so after the career paths that each of them had chosen. He knew that if ever anything happened to one of them, the other would be there to take care of the problem, to rescue him. But he had been right there when Todd needed him, and Jimmy hadn't been able to save him. He hadn't been able to do anything.

It was Todd's wife who finally convinced Jimmy to stay with the department.

"You know it's what he would want you to do," she had told him. "You're too good a firefighter to let Slick Perkins make your decisions for you. He's the one who did this, and you had nothing to do with Todd's dying. His life was over the moment Slick grabbed that knife and…"

It was hard for either of them to talk about Perkins, especially several months later when he was released from jail on a technicality. "Under the influence of mind-altering substances," or something equally ridiculous. Steve had told Jimmy that Perkins was out of jail and had left Rock Hill, afraid that he might have a big target on his back because of what he had done to Todd Bryant. He was right about that.

"All units respond to 67 Spurgis Alley. Residential fire with possible entrapment."

Jimmy's unit was just returning from a false alarm and took the call. They were only a few minutes from the address, a dead-end street off Cranford Road.

Cranford Road. Jimmy shivered as they approached the burning clapboard structure.

EMS 1 arrived a moment later, as well as two police cruisers. A group of curious onlookers milled beneath a spreading oak tree.

"Anybody inside?" one of the police officers asked the crowd, pointing to the smoke-engulfed house.

No one volunteered any information. Finally, a teenage boy emerged from the crowd and pointed to the edge of the yard and a beat-up Oldsmobile station wagon, rusting away in a clump of weeds. Against the front passenger door slumped a disheveled and confused young man—barely out of his teens and a stranger to bath or shower. He was coughing, and his breaths came in rapid, uneven gasps.

Steve and his partner raced over to the victim and immediately noticed the singed hair of his blotchy beard.

"That's a problem." Steve pointed at the charred nose-hairs of the man's nostrils. "Smoke inhalation, and probably heat damage to his lungs. We need to get him to the hospital."

"Anybody else inside?" the officer addressed the teenager again. "He the only one?"

The boy shrugged his shoulders. A man standing behind him grabbed his shirt and pulled him into the crowd, out of sight.

"Let's go," Jimmy told his crew.

Fire hoses were already threading their way from the engine, across the yard, and around the small building. Water was pouring onto the roof and through broken windows as Jimmy and another fireman bashed in the front door and entered the house.

The place was filled with smoke, and their visibility was almost nonexistent. Jimmy's partner pointed to a smoldering mattress in the corner of the living room—the probable starting point of this conflagration.

"I'll check the kitchen," he told Jimmy. "You check that room, and then let's get out of here!"

The kitchen and bathroom were clear, and Jimmy stood in the doorway of the only bedroom. It was filled with smoke as well but devoid of any furniture, and he saw no evidence of another person—or body.

"All clear," his partner called out. "Let's go."

He was out the front door and Jimmy turned to follow. Something caught his eye, and he froze. He was looking in the bathroom. His partner had already cleared the room, but…the bathtub. Something pulled Jimmy into the small space and over to the edge of the stained porcelain fixture. He peered over the edge and…nothing. Empty, except for some old newspapers and a couple of dead mice.

What's wrong with me?

Jimmy turned to the door and once more froze where he stood. Behind the bathroom door, contorted into an impossibly tight bundle, was the outline of a man. And he was breathing.

Jimmy reached down and grabbed him by his shoulder, shaking him vigorously.

"Get up, buddy! We've got to get you out of here!"

In slow motion, the man shifted his body, raised his head, and looked up into the eyes of the fireman.

Jimmy released his grip on the man's shoulder and took a step back. Slick Perkins.

Jimmy Anderson glanced behind him at the empty living room. His partner was long gone, and the house—little more than a pile of kindling—would be totally consumed by flames within a matter of minutes.

He looked at Perkins, whose head now slumped listlessly on his chest. Somewhere in the burning building, a wall collapsed.

Jimmy walked into the break room of the fire station. It was six a.m. and he was just coming on duty. He dropped his lunch bag on the table and turned to his locker.

"Well, if it isn't the local hero!"

His partner was sitting at the table, drinking coffee and finishing off a bagel slathered with cream cheese.

"What are you talking about?" Jimmy fished in his locker without turning around.

"Take a look at this."

Jimmy's head spun around, and his partner slid the morning paper toward him, spinning it so he could read the big, bold headline.

Firefighter Saves Man from Burning Building

Beneath the headline was a picture of Jimmy Anderson...and Slick Perkins.

> *The whole course of human history*
> *may depend on a change of heart*
> *in one solitary and even humble individual—*
> *for it is in the solitary mind and soul*
> *that the battle between good and evil*
> *is waged and either ultimately won or lost.*
>
> M. Scott Peck

22

The Ascent

Sergeant Lenny Burris walked up to the nurses' station and dropped his notepad on the counter. He looked down at it and pushed it away, shaking his head.

"Sometimes it's almost too much to deal with," the police officer lamented. "I've been at this a long time and never been as mad as I am right now."

"What's going on?" Amy Connors asked. "Are you talking about the old man they just took back to Minor Trauma?"

EMS had rolled their stretcher down the hallway a few minutes earlier, carrying an elderly gentleman. His hair was matted with clotted blood, and blood-soaked gauze covered much of his face.

"Yeah, Pete Stevens," Lenny answered. "One of the nicest guys you'd ever want to meet. Vietnam vet. Wife died a couple of years ago, and he lives by himself off Dave Lyle Boulevard. He doesn't deserve something like this."

"What happened to him?" I tossed the chart of room 3 into the discharge basket and picked up Lenny Burris's clipboard. "Seventy-year-old male. Assault—multiple lacerations of face and scalp."

"Pete was just being…Pete, I guess. Minding his own business over at the mall. He was on his way out when he saw two guys messin' with a man in a wheelchair. The man's wife was trying to help him get back in their van when these two men walked up, pushed her down, and started punching her husband. According to a couple of witnesses, they were trying to rob him, and when he said he didn't have any money, they started to beat him."

Lenny paused and shook his head. "Ironic, I suppose. The guy in the wheelchair was a vet, just like Pete. Gulf War, I think, and he can't use his legs. Well, Pete dropped what was in his hands and walked as fast as he could over to the van. Turns out the two are well known to the department. Jimmy Deal and Dakota Sky. Bad actors, and not shy about bustin' somebody up if it serves their purposes. But Pete didn't hesitate—just grabbed Dakota and tossed him aside like a sack of potatoes. Pete Stevens is a big man and still strong. But he was no match for those two guys, and pretty soon they had him on the ground. Jimmy Deal was holding his arms and Dakota was beating his face and head with something—a rock, I think."

"What about those witnesses you mentioned, Lenny?" Amy interrupted. "Didn't anybody help?"

"Somebody called 911," the sergeant answered. "But nobody did a thing to help Pete or the other man. They just waited for the police to come…and watched."

After they arrived at the scene, EMS 2 called in the assault: "Elderly male with multiple lacerations. Alert and talking. And his vital signs are stable."

Apparently he hadn't lost consciousness. That was one good thing.

"He's beaten to a bloody pulp, Doc," Lenny told me. "You'll see. It's going to take a while to put him back together."

"What about the two perps?" Amy's voice had a sharp edge of anger. "We've seen that Jimmy Deal guy in here before, and Dakota Sky sounds familiar. You got those jerks, right?"

"Yeah, we got 'em locked up downtown. They stepped up to the big leagues this time though. They're in real trouble."

I picked up Pete Stevens's chart and started down the hallway.

"Doc," Lenny called out.

I turned around and faced the officer.

"Just be prepared."

I wasn't—not for what lay hidden under the gauze bandages covering Pete Stevens's face. I've seen a lot—too much—in my years in the ER. But the wounds left by this vicious attack were the worst I have ever encountered. Deep, jagged lacerations extended down his forehead and through both eyebrows. His left cheek was fileted, and the right side of his mouth was in pieces. Lenny had been right—and I hadn't even begun to examine Pete's scalp.

He struggled and somehow managed to open an eyelid, nearly sealed with a clot of blood.

"Doc, from what I can tell, this is going to take a while. I think we're going to get to know each other before the evening's through."

He was right on both counts. By the time I tied off the last stitch, I knew a lot about Pete Stevens.

It started when I helped the nurse remove his shirt so I could examine his chest. Deal and Dakota might have done more than beat his head and face—which was more than enough. But I needed to be sure there wasn't anything else going on—no chest injury or unannounced stab wound.

I didn't find any other evidence of trauma, only multiple, purple scars on his back and chest that had long ago healed.

I had decided not to ask him about these, but he slowly lifted his right hand and began tracing the long, curved scar that ran from his right shoulder to his left hip.

"Want me to tell you about this one?"

Our eyes met. "I want you to tell me about *all* of them."

Pete set foot in Vietnam at the age of nineteen years, three months, and fourteen days. He wasn't sure about the hours and minutes, but he was positive about this much. And he was positive about the day and his age when he boarded a plane and flew to Clark Air Base in the Philippines and then home. It was the in-between that changed him forever. He was a gunner on a helicopter and flew 14 missions without incident. Several bullet holes in the fuselage were the closest he and his crew had come to something bad happening. But the fifteenth mission was different.

It started off unusual—from the moment the crew walked into the landing area. The mechanics were still working on the motor when the crew tried to board. They were told to wait so the mechanics could be sure everything was okay. That had never happened before, and a member of the team crossed himself.

Finally, just as they were cleared, one member started patting his pants pockets. He looked around and hollered that he had forgotten something and had to go back to the barracks. It was his good-luck coin.

Too late. Pete and another crewmate grabbed him by his arms and shoved him into the helicopter. Thirty minutes later they were hovering over the safe zone, checking coordinates for the day's mission—support for a ground assault on a village known to be a center of Vietcong activity. Then they headed southwest and into expected danger.

"It took us 45 minutes to get there, Doc," Pete told me from beneath a blue surgical towel. "I remember it like it was yesterday. Clear blue sky, bright green jungle—it was a beautiful day. You'd never have known there was a war going on right below us—until you noticed your buddy sitting beside you with his gun locked and loaded."

He paused, and I lifted an edge of the towel. "Can you breathe under there, Mr. Stevens?"

"Yes, and it's Pete. Call me Pete. Anyway, I was just thinking about how calm everything was—until it wasn't. Everything around me seemed to explode, and I knew we were hit. The guy beside me grabbed his leg—or what was left of it—and started screaming. We started circling and losing control, but somehow our pilot managed to get us close to a clearing. I didn't think there was much chance we were going to make it. I was sure I was going to die that very moment, but I remember not really being afraid. It was just a fact—something that was going to happen and something I couldn't do anything about. But somehow our pilot managed to stabilize that bird just enough for us to land.

"I grabbed my weapon and was about to jump out when I noticed the edges of the clearing. There were soldiers everywhere, and they weren't ours. Doc, that's when the real fear grabbed me. It hadn't occurred to me yet that we might be captured. I was focused on crashing and wondering how that was going to feel. Then we were surrounded and I was afraid. A million thoughts ran through my head—none of them good. Doc, I was nineteen years old. Nineteen. And I was staring into the barrel of an AK-47 and the face of a Vietcong lieutenant."

I stopped suturing and straightened on the stool. Lori Davidson was standing near the stretcher, and our eyes met. She shook her head.

"Can we take a break for a second, Doc? I need to move my neck a little, and my legs. I get these cramps."

"Sure. What can we do to help?"

Pete squirmed on the stretcher, adjusting his hips and knees. "That's better. Can you hold up that towel and let me move my head around a second?"

I picked up the blue cloth, and he lifted his head and circled his neck a few times. Grinding crunches filled the room, and Lori shuddered.

"Arthritis?" I assumed, putting the towel back over his face.

"No, not arthritis," Pete said matter-of-factly. "Bamboo."

"Bamboo?" Lori echoed.

"Yes, ma'am, bamboo." He reached down and rubbed his right knee. "I don't remember a whole lot right after we landed and I was captured. Punched in the face a couple of times and shoved to the ground. Then it's a blur. A couple of days later I was in a small cell, barely conscious. Hungry, thirsty, and scared. I heard somebody moving around down the hallway—I couldn't see anything and didn't know better, so I called out and asked if he was an American and if he knew where we were. He said, 'Hanoi Hilton. Shut up.'

"That's when it started—the bamboo. It seemed like a split second, and there were a couple of guards in my cell. They started beating me with bamboo rods—first my chest and back and then my knees. For days I could barely walk. Then they beat me on my head and neck. I blacked out, and when I woke up, it was pitch-dark. I was afraid to move and wanted to scream, but I thought of the bamboo and just lay there the rest of the night. That went on every day for nine months. Nine months—until I walked out of that place."

We were silent, and I tried to comprehend what that meant—what that would be like, to be beaten every day. I couldn't, and I didn't know what to say to this man.

"You know, Doc, the French built that prison, and it was called *Hoa Lo*. We were told it meant 'hellhole,' and if that wasn't true, it should have been. Whatever you may have heard about that place and what the American POWs went through, multiply it by a factor of ten. No, a hundred. I would never have made it out of there if it hadn't been for Captain Alan Jeffries. He saved my life and kept me from going crazy."

It was time to reposition his head. We took a break, and he moved around on the stretcher while I stood and stretched. Lori had pulled up a stool and sat by his side.

"Not boring you, am I, ma'am?" He turned his wounded head in her direction.

"Not at all, Pete. I have an uncle who spent time in Vietnam. He was never captured and never had anything happen like…this."

"He's lucky then. And I daresay, he's a good man."

Pete lay back down on the stretcher, got as comfortable as he could, and took a deep breath.

"Ready to go again, Doc."

We had been at it for more than an hour, and there was no end in sight.

"Sure. Let's get back at it."

I started working on one of his eyebrows—trying to piece it back together.

"Tell us about Captain Jeffries," Lori said, dabbing at a trickle of blood that was flowing down his cheek and chin.

"Captain Jeffries…" Pete said slowly. "Like I said, I wouldn't be here today if it wasn't for him. When I could finally stand and walk a little, they let me outside in the open for an hour or so each day. That's when I met the captain. He was 32—only a dozen or so years older than me—but he was like a second father. Took me under his wing the moment we met. Tried to teach me how to act and not get beaten—or at least not as bad. We were all going to be beaten every day. Sometimes two or three times. The captain was trying to be sure I didn't get beat to death. A lot of men *did* in that hellhole. But he was trying to help me."

"What kind of stuff did he tell you?" I asked him.

"Some of the things you see in the movies—don't look a guard straight in the eye, don't ever make a threatening motion, keep your mouth shut. Those things seemed obvious but were still hard to keep in mind. Sometimes harder to do. I was in there nine months, and for nine months I was scared to death. And for nine months I was mad as fire, mainly because of what they were doing to me but also because of what those guards were doing to the other soldiers in there.

"Anyway, those were the basic things, like keeping your mouth shut. But the captain taught me how to give a little bow whenever I could. Now, that was hard for me—it felt like some kind of surrender or giving in. But once I learned to do it, it saved me a bunch of beatings. And then he told me never to raise my voice, but to speak softly. Another of those signs of respect, even though none of us had any respect for those people. And there were a bunch of little things, like how to position your hands and shoulders. Yeah, even the way you held your shoulders was important. Just like learning to take a half step back every once in a while. Like I said, he taught me all those things and saved me a lot of pain."

I looked at Lori and shook my head. Trying to survive in that kind of environment was incomprehensible to me.

"But there were two things he did for me—two things I'll never forget. One day we were out in the yard, and for no reason this guard walks up behind me and starts beating me with his bamboo rod. No reason at all…not that they ever needed one. I just stood there and took it, but when he hit me on the head, I almost blacked out and fell to my knees. Boy, let me tell you, when that happened, it was like a swarm of yellow jackets lookin' for a target. Four or five guards rushed at me with their rods and started beating me. I had watched one man die this way, and I was sure it was my time. But the captain jumped in their way and stood between me and them. You can imagine what happened then. They stopped beating me and grabbed the captain and disappeared into their barracks. We didn't see him for two weeks, and when we finally did, he couldn't walk. And could barely talk. His jaw was broken, and three of the fingers on his left hand were all twisted and dislocated. They never were right after that."

Pete stopped, and his chest heaved. His next words were soft—barely audible. "He saved my life that day. All the other stuff was a big help— all of his advice. But if he hadn't stood between me and those guards, I would have died right there in the dirt.

"That's why you're stitchin' me up tonight, Doc. If I ever see someone needing help, someone being picked on or something like that, I'm going to step in and stop them. Like earlier, when I saw those two guys punching the vet, and him in a wheelchair. All of a sudden I was back in that prison and knew I had to stop it—no matter what the cost. The captain never thought about the cost, what stepping in was going to cost him. Didn't matter. That's what he was going to do."

We were quiet for a moment, and I tried to take all of this in.

"You said there were two things Captain Jeffries did for you that you especially remember," Lori reminded him. "What was the other?"

"The other? Hmm…that was the most important. Even more important than saving my life. It was all about this." He raised his right hand and lightly tapped the center of his chest. "It was about my heart—but more importantly it was about my soul. He gave me Psalm 121. He had it memorized, word for word, and he taught it to me."

"I will lift up my eyes to the hills," Lori began.

"Good for you, ma'am."

His face was still covered, and Pete reached out blindly with his hand, searching. Lori took it with both of hers and leaned closer to the stretcher.

"That's one of the 'ascent songs,' you know," Pete explained. "Well, you might not know that, 'cause I didn't. The captain explained that it was in the group of ascent songs because the Jewish people would sing it as they ascended the mountains on the way to the temple. It was a hard journey, and singing kept them focused, I suppose. Helped them to keep going and not give up hope. Finish the journey—the ascent. That's why he gave it to me…so that I wouldn't lose focus. So that I would finish the journey and get out of that place someday."

Lori squeezed his hand. "Your Captain Jeffries must have been a very special man. Have you been able to stay in touch with him?"

The stretcher shuddered gently, and I moved back, looking down. Pete Stevens was sobbing quietly. I didn't say anything, but waited. When he spoke, sadness and tears were in his voice.

"We heard about the Paris peace talks and that President Nixon was getting us out of Vietnam. That was three days before my cell door opened and I was told to get out—to leave. We couldn't believe it. And when we walked down the hallway, I was looking for the captain. I didn't see him, and when I passed by his cell, it was empty. I thought he might have gotten out earlier since he was an officer and all. But my heart told me something different. Two weeks later, I found out the guards had beaten him again—this time to death. And only a couple of days before we all got out. He had saved my life—taught me how to endure that nightmare—and I wasn't there to help him. Not when he needed me."

Lori's voice was quiet, calm. "Mr. Stevens, I believe Captain Jeffries knew what you needed all those years ago—what we all need even today. We need to rest in the sureness that the Lord is watching over us, just like he was watching over you and the captain, and like the captain was watching over you."

I stopped my suturing. Somehow, in the midst of the bloody towels on his face and the blood-soaked gauze littering the floor, a quiet peace filled the room. It was coming from the heart and soul of this unusual and brave man.

"Just like you were watching over that man this afternoon, Pete," I told him. "The captain would be proud of the man that 19-year-old became."

"I hope so, Doc. I hope so."

I lift up my eyes to the mountains—
where does my help come from?
My help comes from the L ORD*,*
the Maker of heaven and earth.
He will not let your foot slip—
he who watches over you will not slumber;
indeed, he who watches over Israel
will neither slumber nor sleep.
The L ORD *watches over you—*
the L ORD *is your shade at your right hand;*
the sun will not harm you by day,
nor the moon by night…
The L ORD *will watch over your coming and going*
both now and forevermore.

P SALM 121

My mother died when I was 14. At her funeral, a hymn was sung, the words of which have forever been seared on my heart.

Abide with me; fast falls the eventide;
the darkness deepens; Lord, with me abide.
When other helpers fail and comforts flee
Help of the helpless, oh, abide with me.

H ENRY F RANCIS L YTE

There will come a time when our helpers will fail and our comforts flee. But there is One who will never fail us, One who will never flee, One who brings life and hope.

Do not fear, for I am with you;
do not be dismayed, for I am your God.
I will strengthen you and help you;
I will uphold you with my righteous right hand.

I SAIAH 41:10

More Great Harvest House Books
by Dr. Robert Lesslie

Angels in the ER

Angels on Call

Angels and Heroes

Angels on the Night Shift

Miracles in the ER

Notes from a Doctor's Pocket

60 Ways to Lower Your Cholesterol

60 Ways to Lower Your Blood Pressure

60 Ways to Lose 10 Pounds (or More)

To learn more about Harvest House books and
to read sample chapters, visit our website:

www.harvesthousepublishers.com

HARVEST HOUSE PUBLISHERS
EUGENE, OREGON